The Wars of the Roses

A Captivating Guide to the English Civil Wars That Brought down the Plantagenet Dynasty and Put the Tudors on the Throne

Free Bonus from Captivating History (Available for a Limited time)

Hi History Lovers!

Now you have a chance to join our exclusive history list so you can get your first history ebook for free as well as discounts and a potential to get more history books for free! Simply visit the link below to join.

Captivatinghistory.com/ebook

Also, make sure to follow us on:

Twitter: @Captivhistory

Facebook: Captivating History:@captivatinghistory

Contents

Introduction

The Wars of the Roses were a complex set of battles, skirmishes, and kidnappings during the 15th century in England. They had their roots in the nearby Civil War of France, which greatly influenced English politics for years to come. Though there is no one universally-accepted start or end date for these wars, the major events throughout the wars occurred between 1455 and 1485.

The central reason for the Wars of the Roses, otherwise referred to as the 15th century English Civil War, was a tug-of-war between two families for the throne of England. Though both families were in fact closely related, they had split half a century earlier. Instead of one unified Plantagenet family, the cousins became Lancasters and Yorks. While the Lancasters remained on the throne, the Yorks were overlooked in the succession of kings. The Yorks became jealous, given their equal relation to England's ancient monarchy, and when the Plantagenet-Lancaster dynasty appeared tragically weakened by the succession of Henry VI, the royal cousins took the opportunity to demand a new ruler.

Henry VI took over the rule of England upon the death of his father when he was not yet one year old. A scramble over leadership in the boy's appointed Regency Council led to the prominence first of Henry's Lancaster uncles, then Richard of York. Upon Henry's coming of age, Richard of York was unwilling to give up his power and under many pretenses he raised an army.

Over the course of several decades, the royalist army and rebel armies fought throughout the country. Led first by Richard of York, then by his son Edward of York, the rebels gained and lost the power of the crown multiple times, as of course did the royal Plantagenet-Lancaster side. Fighting continued until both sides eventually lost their grip on the crown into the hands of the founder of a brand-new royal dynasty.

Chapter 1 – A Short History of the House of Plantagenet

Every history buff knows who the Tudors were. But what about the dynastic family who ruled England for nearly 300 years before the Tudors had even left Wales, seeking greatness beyond the borders of their homeland? The Plantagenets were the English monarchs who took control of a confused and fractious nation after the Norman Conquest and smoothed down the roughest of its edges. They were violent, heavy-handed, and lacked even a hint of the highly-touted civility and gentleness of later eras. Yet, without their brute force, England and Great Britain would be very different today.

European history is rife with long-lived family names, each one heavy with the weight of centuries of nobility, war, and royal entanglement. The name "Tudor," "York," or "Plantagenet" calls up images of swords, throne rooms, and the heavy golden livery collars of people who helped shape history. It may be surprising to learn that the historical surname, or House, of Plantagenet began its infamous life as a simple nickname for conqueror Geoffrey V d'Anjou. In the 12th century, d'Anjou was the powerful Duke of Normandy and count of several domains within modern France.

Historians hypothesize that the name "Plantagenet" was given to Geoffrey because of the yellow straw-like flowers he wore in his hat, which were named "plantagenets." Whatever the reason for the moniker, Geoffrey V d'Anjou is considered the founder of House Plantagenet, which was also referred to as the Order of Anjou before the Tudor era. The Plantagenet title was not actually used in reference to Geoffrey and his descendants until the reign of Henry VII. It was a purely retroactive House denomination created simply to refer to the ruling dynasty that came before Henry Tudor and his descendants. By the 17th century, the term was commonplace and fully accepted by historians and royal genealogists who had become used to this type of familial departmentalization.

The original Plantagenet, Geoffrey, was a continental Norman who married into the English royal family in 1128 to King Henry I's daughter, Matilda. It was a political marriage arranged primarily by Henry I, who wanted to cement the aging ties between Normandy and the English descendants of Normandy's William the Conqueror. Both England and Normandy were politically tied, but their administration was not centralized until Henry I pushed leaders in both regions to pledge their loyalties to his daughter.

Despite Henry I's best efforts to protect his crown for Matilda, it was taken by his nephew, Stephen of Blois, after his death in 1135. King Stephen had many supporters, but so did Matilda and the Duke of Anjou. The usurpation of the throne caused civil war in 1139 when Geoffrey Plantagenet and Matilda marched into London with an army and took the crown by force. Only a few years later, Stephen stole his position back and the deposed rulers fled to Normandy.

By that time, Plantagenet was the ruler of Normandy, so the family remained there. The couple had three sons together, one of whom would inherit England: Henry II. When Henry II became king, it marked the beginning of a three-century dynasty of Plantagenets that didn't end until Richard III's death in 1485.

The Duke of Anjou gifted the kingdom to his son Henry in 1150. Henry married Eleanor of Aquitaine, thereby gaining control of most of France, and then invaded England twice before securing the right to succeed to the throne following the death of King Stephen. Henry II became the King of England in 1154.

King Henry II began his rule by attempting to erase the legacy of his predecessor. He required the noble houses of England to destroy all castles they had built for Stephen. The new king established the federal finance ministry and brought back the royal justices, whose job it was to travel throughout the kingdom and judge criminal cases.

Descendants of Geoffrey Plantagenet and Henry II were often at war and at odds with the nobility or the Papacy, but they held tight to the fundamental principles that kept the country's economy running – taxation and the implementation of localized law and order.

The Plantagenet dynasty was a formative era for England and the future United Kingdom. Geoffrey Plantagenet's successors oversaw the formation of an English Parliament, the official institutionalization of feudalism, the domination of Wales, and several political alliances with Scotland following the rebellions of William Wallace. It was during the Plantagenet era that England and France embarked upon the Hundred Years' War, an era of constant land disputes that usually involved the continental regions of Aquitaine, Normandy, Brittany, Anjou, and Maine – most of the regions Henry II and his wife Eleanor held in their possession. Both England and France had reason to believe these places fell under their own jurisdiction, and neither was willing to permanently concede defeat.

Though the Plantagenet family did indeed rule England from the 12th century, the dynasty was split into two factions of cousins in 1399. That year, following the death of John of Gaunt, the Plantagenet line broke into two separate sub-houses: Lancaster and York. Both retained an equal relationship with John of Gaunt, heir to King Edward III, meaning both had a solid claim to the throne. The controversy between the cousins came about due to which heir on which side was closest to the previous monarch. In a family feud over the crown that lasted 86 years, it was these Lancasters and Yorks who were responsible for bringing England to civil war in the 15th century.

The Lancasters retained the throne after the death of King Edward III, while the Yorks were installed in important positions at court and throughout the kingdom. Balance held, though delicately, and both sides of the family developed their own identity. The Lancasters adopted the red rose as their sigil, while the Yorks adopted the white rose. In the 15th century, the Yorks usurped the English throne from the Lancaster king, and the two sets of roses declared war upon each other.

Chapter 2 – Civil War in France

Though the English Civil War did not break out until King Henry VI reached adulthood, the most prominent factor behind the future Wars of the Roses was the succession of this child. Upon the death of Lancastrian King Henry V while campaigning in France, the nine-month-old heir became king of England in his stead in August of 1422. Just months later, the infant king's grandfather, French King Charles VI, died, having made England's rulers the rightful heirs to France. Not yet a year in age, Henry VI was the ruler of all England and France.

The young king's mother, Catherine of Valois, was the daughter of the deceased French king, which could have made her a very powerful regent. However, Parliament stepped in to create a Regency Council that excluded Catherine and appointed only men. The council was comprised of 18 people, including John of Lancaster and Humphrey of Lancaster, who were the most prominent councilors of the group since they were brothers of the old king and uncles of the new. John went to France to govern the English lands abroad while Humphrey stayed in England as Lord Protector of the Realm.

The most controversial issue facing Henry VI's Regency Council was the ongoing Hundred Years' War with France. Though England's own monarch was, in name, the King of France, it was impossible for the English to govern an entire country in which there were immense forces aimed against foreign rule. The disinherited son of the old French king, Charles Valois, garnered great support for his cause and waged civil war against the English and their French allies. Infamous patriotic warrior, Jean d'Arc, joined the fight on the side of Charles VII, changing the momentum of the war.

Charles VII was crowned king of France at Reims Cathedral in 1429. Charles built on this victory by adding more soldiers to his forces and more districts of France to his own group of allies. They fought hard against the English but had much ground to recover, which was particularly difficult given that Charles was still not accepted by all French provinces as their king. Jean d'Arc herself wrote to the English king and his council, asking them to give up France to the French or suffer the consequences:

> *King of England, render account to the King of Heaven of your royal blood. Return the keys of all the good cities which you have seized, to the Maid. She is sent by God to reclaim the royal blood, and is fully prepared to make peace, if you will give her satisfaction; that is, you must render justice, and pay back all that you have taken.*

> *King of England, if you do not do these things, I am the commander of the military; and in whatever place I shall find your men in France, I will make them flee the country, whether they wish to or not; and if they will not obey, the Maid will have them all killed. She comes sent by the King of Heaven, body for body, to take you out of France, and the Maid promises and certifies to you that if you do not leave France she and her troops will raise a mighty outcry as has not been heard in France in a thousand years. And believe that the King of Heaven has sent her so much power that you will not be able to harm her or her brave army.*

To you, archers, noble companions in arms, and all people who are before Orleans, I say to you in God's name, go home to your own country; if you do not do so, beware of the Maid, and of the damages you will suffer. Do not attempt to remain, for you have no rights in France from God, the King of Heaven, and the Son of the Virgin Mary. It is Charles, the rightful heir, to whom God has given France, who will shortly enter Paris in a grand company. If you do not believe the news written of God and the Maid, then in whatever place we may find you, we will soon see who has the better right, God or you.

William de la Pole, Count of Suffolk, Sir John Talbot, and Thomas, Lord Scales, lieutenants of the Duke of Bedford, who calls himself regent of the King of France for the King of England, make a response, if you wish to make peace over the city of Orleans! If you do not do so, you will always recall the damages which will attend you.

Duke of Bedford, who call yourself regent of France for the King of England, the Maid asks you not to make her destroy you. If you do not render her satisfaction, she and the French will perform the greatest feat ever done in the name of Christianity.

Done on the Tuesday of Holy Week (March 22, 1429).

HEAR THE WORDS OF GOD AND THE MAID.

The Regency Council thought little of France's beloved female knight and continued its fight on the continent for another 15 years before an armistice was agreed upon in 1444.

King Henry VI turned 16 in 1437, finally coming of age to rule his kingdoms. He took over England and England-allied France from his Regency Council, at which point it became known as his Privy Council. The English privy councilors were split between a desire for peace and a desire to press onward in France. Richard

Plantagenet, a York cousin of the king, had taken one of the coveted Regency positions just one year prior to the king's birthday; he strongly favored continued military efforts abroad.

The acting king, however, was not in favor of continued fighting. He wanted to put an end to the Hundred Years' War and come to some kind of final agreement between England and France, whatever that may mean for England's holdings abroad. Haste would have been ideal, since the Royal Treasury was in deep debt from war expenses. The king was no match for his political rival, Richard of York, however. Richard was a powerful force within the council, and so war continued, less and less to England's advantage.

King Henry VI was not without his own strategy, however. He worked together with his favorite advisor, William de la Pole, to put a stop to the war and restore peace in France. De la Pole organized the Treaty of Tours, intended as the armistice of 1444. It was signed by Henry VI and Charles VII and laid out the stipulations of marriage between the English king and a member of the French aristocracy. France asked Henry VI to give up his claim to the French throne, offering him several regions in the south of France as motivation to do so. He also demanded the return of Anjou and Maine to French control. Charles VII was unwilling to give England any territories without maintaining ultimate ownership, so these negotiations wore on without ever reaching a firm conclusion.

Arrangement of the meeting between envoys of the kings was lengthy and perpetually delayed, as letters between courts show:

> *Instructions to the ambassadors sent by the king of France and the duke of Orleans to the earl of Suffolk to arrange a meeting at which to discuss the terms of peace between France and England.*

> *In the first place, the said lord de Gancort, Guichart and Aude, shall tell them, upon the part of the king, how, three weeks ago, or thereabouts, my said lord of Orleans caused it to be intimated that the said earl of Suffolk had written to him*

by Valois, his herald, who was coming direct from England, that he and others of the said embassy would land shortly at Calais, and would come into the marches in that neighbourhood. And upon this occasion, the king immediately appointed certain men of mark of his own, to meet those of the said embassy, in order to conduct and bring them to the place of Compiegne, or some other locality in the neighbourhood of the river of Seine, to which place he had arranged that my said lord of Orleans should proceed. And likewise he directed that his chancellor and other notable people of his council and of his court of parliament should betake themselves from that side to those of the said embassy in order to advise with them, and further to arrange with them in the matter above-said, as well expedient. And he took care to send a message to Monseigneur de Bourgogne that he would dispatch some of his people, as well to guide the said embassy through his territories, as to accompany my said lord of Orleans and Monseigneur the chancellor, so that the said embassy should be conducted. And the king took care to send Guillem Beslier, his bailly of Troys, to my said lord, the chancellor, in order diligently to prepare and to accomplish what has been specified.

...Since the king is still somewhat weak in his person by occasion of a certain accidental malady which he had lately had, and also because it was expected that the said embassy would land upon the side of Calais, as is said, the people of my said lord of Bourgogne have, in consequence, not yet arrived here, but it is probable that they will immediately proceed to the said marches towards Calais; and also because my said lord the chancellor for the causes aforesaid is still in the marches near Paris, and it is very fitting that he should be present to give heed to these matters; therefore it appears to my said lord of Orleans that it is expedient to make a journey after this feast of Easter in order to cause the *said embassy to come into some place which holds with the king, to begin and give attention in the matter above-said.*

De la Pole would be blamed for negotiations that failed England in favor of France, though he acted on his king's orders and stated he had promised nothing concrete to Charles VII. While the ownership of several French regions, including Anjou, Maine, and Brittany were still under negotiations, the marriage contract between countries held strong.

In 1445, the king married Margaret of Anjou, the Princess of Naples, in-law of Charles VII, member of the French House of Anjou, and daughter to the Duchess of Lorraine. The Duchy of Lorraine was officially part of the Holy Roman Empire, but at the time of Margaret's wedding, it was effectively ruled by members of the House Valois. The marriage was the keystone to Henry VI's plan for peace between the Valois and Plantagenet families, and by extension, France and England. At the time of the wedding, Henry was 23 years old and Margaret was 15.

Originally, the Treaty of Tours promised 21 months of peace between the two countries, but the treaty was extended at the insistence of Henry VI. The king believed that his marriage and a long-term peace treaty would cement affable relations between the two countries, but his plan didn't succeed. In 1448, Charles VII threatened England with warfare if Maine and Anjou were not handed back to the French; King Henry VI did so, but it did not halt the onslaught of war. Fighting resumed in 1450, and Valois' forces defeated the English in several crucial battles, pushing them out of France and ultimately out of their own continental French strongholds, except for Calais. By mid-century, the Hundred Years' War had all but ended, with England on the losing side.

England's loss signaled the end of the French Civil War, and the beginning of the wars at home.

Chapter 3 – England's Loss and a King's Illness

Several important events occurred during the final years of the Hundred Years' War. One of Henry's uncles, the Duke of Bedford, died. The wife of his remaining uncle, Humphrey Plantagenet, was found guilty of performing witchcraft intended to bring on the death of the king. She was forced to divorce Humphrey, the Duke of Gloucester, and live in prison for the remainder of her life.

Soon after King Henry's marriage to Margaret of Anjou, the new queen became suspicious of her husband's uncle, the Duke of Gloucester. Humphrey Plantagenet stood to inherit the throne of England upon the death of Henry VI, a fact that the queen felt certain he would take advantage of. The king was convinced that his uncle plotted against him, which may or may not have been a reality, and Humphrey was arrested. He died only a few days later in prison in 1447.

In 1450, King Henry VI's most influential councilor, the Duke of Suffolk (William de la Pole) was scapegoated by the rest of the council as the reason England lost its lands in France. The king was forced to banish him from England. Upon making his exit to the mainland, Suffolk was intercepted and decapitated by an angry mob.

That same year, Jack Cade, a northern Yorkist from Kent, published his Proclamation of Grievances. He believed, as did Richard of York, that the king had surrounded him with poor counsel and was not personally heeding the laws of the land.

> *These be the points, cause and mischiefs of gathering and assembling of us, the king's liege men of Kent, the 4th day of June the year of our Lord 1450, the reign of our sovereign lord the king 29th, which we trust to Almighty God to remedy, with the help and the grace of God and of our sovereign lord the king, and the poor commons of England, and else we shall die therefore: We, considering that the king our sovereign lord, by the insatiable, covetous, malicious persons that daily and nightly are about his highness, and daily inform him that good is evil and evil is good:*
>
> *Item. They say that our sovereign is above his laws to his pleasure, and he may make it and break it as he pleases, without any distinction. The contrary is true, or else he should not have sworn to keep it.*
>
> *Item. They say that the commons of England would first destroy the king's friends and afterward himself, and then bring the Duke of York to be king so that by their false means and lies they may make him to hate and destroy his friends, and cherish his false traitors. They call themselves his friends, and if there were no more reason in the world to know, he may know they be not his friends by their covetousness.*
>
> *Item. They say that it were great reproof to the king to take again what he has given, so that they will not suffer him to have his own good, nor land, nor forfeiture, nor any other good but they ask it from him, or else they take bribes of others to get it for him.*
>
> *Item. It is to be remedied that the false traitors will suffer no man to come into the king's presence for no cause without bribes where none ought to be had. Any man might have his coming to him to ask him grace or judgment in such case as the king may give.*
>
> *Item. They say that whom the king wills shall be traitor, and whom he wills shall be not, and that appears hitherto, for if any of the traitors about him would malign against any person, high or low, they would find false many that should die a traitor for to have his lands and his goods, but they will suffer the king neither to pay his debts withal, nor pay for his victuals nor be the richer of one penny.*
>
> *Item. The law serves of nought else in these days but for to do wrong, for nothing is spread almost but false matters by color of the law for reward,*

dread and favor and so no remedy is had in the Court of Equity in any way.

Item. We say our sovereign lord may understand that his false council has lost his law, his merchandise is lost, his common people is destroyed, the sea is lost, France is lost, the king himself is so set that he may not pay for his meat nor drink, and he owes more than ever any King of England ought, for daily his traitors about him where anything should come to him by his laws, anon they take it from him.

Item. They ask gentlemen's goods and lands in Kent and call them rioters, and traitors and the king's enemies, but they shall be found the king's true liege men and best friends with the help of Jesus, to whom we cry day and night with many thousand more that God of His grace and righteousness shall take vengeance and destroy the false governors of his realm that has brought us to naught and into much sorrow and misery.

Item. We will that all men know we blame not all the lords, nor all those that are about the king's person, nor all gentlemen nor yeomen, nor all men of law, nor all bishops, nor all priests, but all such as may be found guilty by just and true inquiry and by the law.

Item. We will that it be known we will not rob, nor plunder, nor steal, but that these defaults be amended, and then we will go home; wherefore we exhort all the king's true liege men to help us, to support us, for whatsoever he be that will not that these defaults be amended, he his falser than a Jew or Saracen.

Item. His true commons desire that he will remove from him all the false progeny and affinity of the Duke of Suffolk and to take about his noble person his true blood of his royal realm, that is to say, the high and mighty prince the Duke of York, exiled from our sovereign lord's person by the noising of the false traitor, the Duke of Suffolk, and his affinity. Also to take about his person the mighty prince, the Duke of Exeter, the Duke of Buckingham, the Duke of Norfolk, and his true earls and barons of his land, and he shall be the richest king Christian.

Item. Where we move and pray that some true justice with certain true lords and knights may be sent into Kent for to inquire of all such traitors and bribers, and that the justice may do upon our sovereign lord direct his letters patent to all the people there universal openly to be read and cried, that it is our sovereign lord's will and prayer of all his people truly to inquire of every man's government and of defaults that reign, neither for love, favor, dread, nor hate, and that due judgment shall be forthwith and thereupon.

Without Suffolk, Henry VI came to depend heavily upon his wife, Margaret of Anjou. Margaret was young, but she was clever, ambitious, and trusted by her husband. As it became clear that King Henry was not only a weak ruler but that he suffered from bouts of psychological instability, Margaret's role as queen of England grew less supportive and more vital. She knew, given Henry's mental illness, that the crown was in constant danger from close rivals. After the death of the Duke of Gloucester, that threat came in the form of Richard Plantagenet, also called Richard of York.

Richard Plantagenet was given a position on the Great Council, an emergency authoritative council created in 1453 at the onset of Henry VI's first major illness. After having heard that the last of his English forces had been pushed out of France, the king became mute and ceased to govern. The Great Council tried to make do, hoping the illness would be short-lived, but it proved a lengthy battle. The next year, the Great Council elected Richard of York as Lord Protector of the Realm.

Margaret of Anjou was not pleased with this promotion, since Richard Plantagenet arguably had a firmer claim to the throne of England than did her own husband. Both Henry and Richard were direct descendants of King Edward III; however, Richard's birth was a generation closer to his great-grandfather than Henry was to the same great-great-grandfather.

Richard of York did indeed want to claim the English crown, but his life and ambitions depended on pretending that he was a firm supporter of Henry VI.

The first order of business for the newly-appointed Lord Protector of the Realm was to imprison his biggest competition and friend to the king and queen, the Duke of Somerset. Unfortunately for Richard, Margaret gave birth that same year, 1453, to Prince Edward. By 1455, King Henry VI was ready to rule once more, so Richard of York was set aside, and Somerset freed from prison.

No longer directly in line to the throne nor in charge of the kingdom, Richard Plantagenet took matters into his own hands and called together an army. He met King Henry VI with Queen Margaret, Somerset, and other allies traveling north near St. Albans and attacked them. Somerset and 300 others were killed. Henry VI was wounded and taken hostage by the York faction.

A strange and drawn-out civil war had officially begun.

Chapter 4 – Treason by the Duke of York

The Battle of St. Albans was a clear victory for the Yorkists, but it was not their goal to kill the king. They wanted only to subdue him and keep him in their possession. Since there was already an heir apparent in Henry's son Edward, the king's death would have likely led to another regency council headed by the boy's powerful and influential mother. Probably only for this reason, Henry VI was captured but largely unharmed.

When Richard of York took Henry VI back to London the next day, he did so under the pretense that he was once again acting as the king's regent. York had his royal hostage kept comfortably in a variety of castles and apparently Henry did very little complaining about his circumstances. Months later, when the king's Parliament held a rare meeting, it was informed by York that Henry was once more unfit for the throne. The Parliament declared Richard of York the Protector of England, a title he held until early 1456 when Henry once more rallied and joined his council. Instead of punishing his captor, Henry reinstated York as a leader of his army and commissioned him to respond against regular threats at the Scottish border. York was also made Lieutenant of Ireland and spent most of his time in that part of the realm.

Henry's desire for peaceful relations with all factions was strong, a fact clearly exemplified by his forgiving treatment of Richard of York. Henry organized a meeting between his kidnapper, York's in-laws the Nevilles, and the crown's own representatives. This was a classic medieval-style cease-fire, known as a Loveday. The meeting took place on March 24, 1458. Negotiations were made between all parties, and ultimately the Lancasters, Yorks, and all their major allies agreed to maintain peace and forgive one another for real or imagined trespasses. Though King Henry was proud of the affair, to most involved, the event was considered largely ceremonial.

Margaret of Anjou, for her part, had begun to believe that her husband was incapable of protecting his position and dealing with threats to himself and his family. Fortunately for Henry and their children, the Queen of England was a strong and intelligent woman. She took a firm hand with her husband for both their sakes. Margaret knew that despite the illusion of friendship and forgiveness between the two Plantagenet lines on Loveday, there were armed forces at the ready on both sides. The next summer, Margaret called for a Great Council meeting to which Richard of York and his main allies in the Neville family were not invited. York and his supporters knew what this meant—they were about to be accused of treason.

Before the council met, Richard recruited as many fighting men to his cause as he could with the help of the Nevilles. On the royal Lancaster side, Margaret of Anjou personally recruited soldiers to fill her army ranks, gathering twice as many as the rebels. The first clash between the two armies came at the Battle of Blore Heath in Staffordshire on September 23, 1459. Part of the Yorkist army marched south to join the rest of Richard's forces, and the royal army met them before they could complete the journey.

The Lancaster army had around 10,000 men assembled, whereas the incomplete York army had only 5,000. A creek passed between the two armies with deep banks that made forging the water a tricky endeavor, and to avoid needless fighting, the leaders of the armies, Lord Aubrey for the Lancasters and the Duke of Salisbury for the

Yorks, attempted to find a diplomatic solution. Ultimately, they failed to do so. Both sides advanced.

Despite having all possible advantages, the royal army was besieged into retreat under vicious attacks from the rebels. Lord Aubrey was killed, as well as 2,000 of his soldiers. Hundreds of royalists switched sides mid-battle, which probably had more to do with saving their own lives than it did with their political beliefs. Under the secondary leadership of Lord Dudley, the Lancaster army fled, leaving Salisbury to continue southward and join Richard of York.

Less than a month later, still awaiting reinforcements from Salisbury in the north and Lord Warwick in Calais, the Duke of York and his partial army occupied Ludlow along the Welsh border. They'd been pushed back from London by the king's forces and knew they'd need full numbers before it would be possible to enter the capital city.

Richard, his father and Richard Neville (the Earl of Warwick) arrived with their troops in mid-October to face the royal army as it approached with the king himself at its head in full armor. It was a surprising moment for many of York's assembled soldiers since Richard had insisted that his fight was not against the king, but the king's advisors.

When Henry VI offered pardons to anyone in the Yorkist army willing to switch sides, all 600 men from Calais joined the Lancaster troops. York, Warwick and Salisbury fled, pretending to return to Ludlow for a night of discussion but actually deserting their own soldiers. They ran to Wales, leaving the army facing the king without any leadership. There was no alternative for the rebel troops except to kneel to Henry, which they did. York's family was taken into custody.

Despite the lack of any large-scale fighting, this stand-off came to be known as the Battle of Ludford Bridge. It momentarily cemented King Henry VI's place on the throne, both in the minds of the rebels and the royal supporters. The Lancastrians returned home to enjoy their victory as Henry and Margaret's enemies fled. Once safe at a distance in Wales, York returned to Ireland and Warwick to Calais. Parliament, at long last, denounced the Duke of York as a traitor.

Amazingly, Richard Plantagenet had not yet run out of supporters. Warwick and Salisbury would return to England to battle the king's forces again the very next year.

Chapter 5 – The Battle of Northampton

In the spring of 1460, Warwick sailed from Calais once more to meet Salisbury in Ireland and make plans for their upcoming attack. Both had garnered more support for York's claim to the throne, particularly in Ireland where the younger Richard had served as Lieutenant for several years. Though King Henry had named a new Lieutenant of Ireland in place of Richard and a new Captain of Calais in place of Neville, citizens of Ireland and Calais did not recognize any authority but that of the old leaders.

York decided to stay in Ireland, safe, while the Nevilles led the attack on Henry VI's troops. Warwick and Salisbury did as York commanded, gathering their armies and marching into London at the beginning of July. The city was unsure how to prepare for the onslaught, eventually remaining true to Henry VI and stationing soldiers along the London Bridge to prevent the Yorkists' entrance. Thomas Scales and Robert Hungerford were stationed at the Tower of London with armaments, ready to face a siege. Locked up within the compound were members of the public who could not fight or were unwilling to do so.

The Earl of Salisbury's army broke through the ranks of Lancastrians at the London Bridge but could not penetrate the walls of the Tower. The two sides fought fruitlessly, Scales opting to use the weapons at his disposal to fire into the city. His imprecise bombardment killed many Londoners as well as Yorkists, but the opposing army did not back down. Salisbury continued to press on the walls of the Tower while his son, Earl of Warwick, marched towards Henry and his army at Northampton on July 10.

At Northampton, the royal forces were outnumbered by the rebels, though they did have a few cannons on their side. Warwick sent messengers repeatedly asking to speak with the king but was denied every time, finally being told that an attempted meeting would end in Warwick's death. Neville's final message stated that at two o'clock he would either speak with King Henry VI or die. Promptly at two o'clock, the Yorkist army advanced.

Luck was not with the Lancaster forces, as a steady rain robbed them of their only advantage by soaking the cannons. Worse than the loss of the artillery was the fact that an entire flank of their army had arranged to commit treason on behalf of the rebel faction. Lord Grey of Ruthin was the army leader responsible for letting Warwick's troops through his ranks and into the royal camp, where they seized King Henry. In exchange for giving the king's enemies easy access to the camp, Grey received York's support in a land dispute and was later named Treasurer of England.

Four of Henry's top advisors sacrificed themselves on his behalf, but the king was taken captive for a second time despite their efforts. Three hundred troops were killed at the Battle of Northampton. Afterward, Warwick took Henry VI back to London and his army joined with Salisbury's to insist London's protectors open the gates of the Tower. Scales and Hungerford fought viciously against the attackers but saw the numbers against them were too great to overcome. They were forced to admit a few men with whom to discuss terms of a ceasefire, and the Tower was surrendered to the rebels. Hungerford escaped the city but Scales was captured by his own citizens, furious at his haphazard shooting, and killed.

Following the battle at Northampton, Richard of York believed he'd won the war. He triumphantly re-entered England, heading straight for London. He brought his own council to court, confirmed that Henry VI was caged in the Tower and rode into the city that September under a banner which displayed the Royal Arms of England. When York reached Henry's palace, however, he did not receive the welcome or celebration he had expected. No one hailed him as king, and they refused to do so no matter how plainly he made his case.

The fact was that both Henry VI and his son were alive, and therefore it was only in the hands of Parliament to grant the Duke of York the ultimate position of power. The parliamentarians met and discussed the situation, deciding that it was not for them to put a living king aside. After all, monarchs were considered appointees of God and therefore subordinate only to the administration of the Catholic Church; certainly not to a congregation of politicians.

Parliament did not grant Richard of York the kingship, but it did recognize its potential chance to stop the endless infighting between the two Plantagenet factions. It was obvious that the Duke of York wanted nothing less than ultimate control over England, and without that, he would wage war ceaselessly until he was satisfied. In an attempt to satisfy him, Parliament granted him the ongoing role of Lord Protector of England. At least this way, York would harness the control he desired and England would benefit from having a sane person in possession of Henry VI's power. In addition, York and his progeny were granted the right of succession over Prince Edward of Lancaster. So, when Henry VI died, his son would be overlooked in favor of Richard or Edward of York.

King Henry did not begrudge the slow usurpation of his crown, but instead lamented all the violence and death that went into each attempt to take it. He was a generally complacent prisoner, happy to occupy himself in his own rooms and hope that his obedience saved lives. If he was angry at the Act of Accord, which cut his son out of the succession of kings, he did not make a fuss. Margaret, who had escaped the fighting with young Edward, would make it for him.

Though he was without the title "King of England," Richard Plantagenet held the most prominent position in the kingdom and Henry VI remained locked away in the Tower of London. For several months, the Lord Protector remained in London to organize his affairs. It was not long before his army was needed again.

Chapter 6 – Margaret's Army

After the Battle of Northampton, King Henry was placed under the custody of York's allies and kept away from court. The king's quarters were comfortable and he was well-cared for, though every visitor, letter and move he made were monitored closely by York's enforcers. As before, the king made no attempt to free himself and may not even have considered himself to be in a predicament. In some reports, the king considered his captor a friend and protector and was happy to follow Richard's instructions.

His wife and son escaped the fray unharmed and ran to Wales to avoid being captured by Richard's forces. By this point, Margaret very clearly understood her role within the royal family: matriarch. She was young and not particularly experienced, but she was motivated by the need to take care of her little son and keep herself safe from political enemies. The queen had a loyal contingent that made sure she and young Edward were whisked away even as Henry VI was being captured and placed into the custody of Richard Plantagenet. She was not content to cower behind her guards, however, and started to formulate a plan to win back her family's position.

When she felt it was safe, Margaret traveled with Edward to Scotland to plead for help from Queen Mary of Guelders. Guelders was Scotland's acting regent for her underage son, King James III, and though her country had a constant record of violence and land disputes with England, she recognized the good sense in helping her neighbor queen. The Scottish queen knew that if England's monarchy could be overthrown by its cousins, the same thing could happen in Scotland. Mary of Guelders made the best of the situation and agreed to equip Margaret with troops in exchange for the disputed city of Berwick-upon-Tweed. While the Queen of England negotiated, adding Scots and Welsh troops to her existing English armies, the loyal lords in northern England put together their own armies and took over Richard Plantagenet's key city of York.

The Duke of York had no choice but to ride north from London and face the insurgents. He sent his son Edward to quell the Lancastrian influence in Wales and left the Earl of Warwick in charge of troops in London. On December 21, 1460, York's army arrived at Sandal Castle, his own estate just outside of Wakefield, Yorkshire. He took back and occupied Sandal Castle with troops numbering 5000 to 6000. Meanwhile, Margaret's army traveled south to Yorkshire and set up camp nearby for the week of Christmas. Messengers traveled back and forth between the castle and the Lancastrian camp and a pact of non-violence was agreed over the holiday.

Though Margaret of Anjou was in control of the combined forces of Lancastrians after the Battle of Northampton, she most likely stayed in York or even Scotland while the army did her bidding. Once out of her immediate range, Margaret's army fell under the combined leadership of Henry Beaufort, Henry Percy, Henry Holland and many other family heads close to the Lancasters. Many of these men had lost brothers, fathers and sons in the previous battles and had personal agendas against the Duke of York.

Over the Christmas break, York's forces faced a shortage of supplies and were forced to leave the fortified estate to forage and hunt for food. They were running out of the basic foodstuffs necessary to stay and fight, which may explain York's decisions when the violence commenced.

York's military maneuvers during the ensuing Battle of Wakefield were ultimately a very rapid failure. Richard stayed with his army nine days at Sandal Castle before engaging the enemy, and during that time sent a messenger to ask his son Edward for reinforcements. Neither Edward nor any of his soldiers arrived in time, though there were no major skirmishes between Margaret and Richard until the second-last day of 1460.

On December 30, Margaret commanded her military leaders to approach Sandal Castle and arrange themselves for battle a mile from York's residence. The Lancastrians are said to have outnumbered their enemy perhaps two to one, a fact that helped them spread out through the land with at least three battalions facing the castle. They remained steady, perhaps finalizing the details of their attack, but York beat them to it.

Freshly-supplied with more troops gathered by Lord John Neville, York was ready to face the Lancastrians. Plantagenet kept command of the troops he'd brought to the castle, while Neville maintained command of the troops he'd gathered. While strategizing, Neville convinced the Duke of York to make his stand in the field rather than from within his fortified compound. It was a very poorly-planned move that made little sense to those fighting on either side. As long as Richard held his castle, his soldiers could benefit from the fortification, doors and thick walls of Sandal Castle while forcing his enemies to waste their strength trying to break through. Nevertheless, Richard was buoyed by the arrival of Neville's battalion, possibly influenced by the fact that food was scarce at Sandal Castle, and confident enough to meet the Lancastrians in the field east of Wakefield.

The Yorkists followed their leader out of the compound and towards the line of the enemy. as almost immediately the Yorkists were surrounded on all sides by the royal army. Fighting was fierce and violent, and a section of York's army had clearly agreed beforehand to betray him. Under the leadership of Sir Andrew Trollope, hundreds of Richard Plantagenet's allied soldiers changed allegiance mid-battle, confusing the Yorkists and causing localized chaos that spread through the ranks.

The Battle of Wakefield was the biggest and bloodiest battle of the civil war, though it probably lasted only about an hour. Trollope's turncoat actions made things difficult for York, but the real turning point of the engagement was John Neville's entrance into the fray – on the side of his apparent enemy. It turned out that Neville had distanced himself from York's troops only to give himself room to turn on them and help the Lancastrians surround him. Soon, Richard Plantagenet was killed and the battle finished. Thousands lay dead, including York's son Edmund and John Neville, the man who'd made such a difference the outcome of the battle.

The Lancastrians put the Duke of York's head on a spike next to his son's. They were displayed on the Roman Micklegate Bar in York, Richard's head wearing a paper crown. His body was buried at Pontefract and later reburied at a church in Fotheringhay, the location of Richard's favorite residence. At the end of the 19th century, a monument was erected to mark the fall of Richard Plantagenet at Wakefield.

Because Richard of York had been granted the right of succession by English Parliament, his death meant his remaining son, Edward, was next in line to the throne following the death of King Henry VI. Henry, of course, was still very much alive, though he remained unofficially imprisoned under York's orders in London.

Chapter 7 – Mortimer's Cross and the Battle of Towton

The death of Richard Plantagenet did not bring the civil war to an end. Immediately upon the defeat of his father and brother at the Battle of Wakefield, 18-year-old Edward Plantagenet—also called the Earl of March—took up the Yorkist cause for himself. Neither army could desist and go home, as the battles were by no means finished. Less than a month after the clash at Wakefield, troops began strategic movements on both sides. At this point, the Tudor family joined the war.

Jasper and Owen Tudor, half-brother and step-father to King Henry VI, gathered pro-Lancaster troops in their native Wales before marching into England to confront Edward, the Earl of March. At the beginning of February 1461, the Tudor's army met with the remaining York army, now under the leadership of young Edward VI. The fighting occurred at Mortimer's Cross near Hereford, which had been Edward's stronghold while his father led the Yorkist armies.

The Lancaster forces were ultimately bested by the Yorkists, with the former forced to flee southward. It has been documented that thousands of troops were killed, though historians believe the numbers were not so high. Among the dead was Owen Tudor, husband to dowager queen Catherine of Valois. His son escaped with his life.

Just weeks later, a separate faction of the York army, led by the Earl of Warwick, fought Margaret's army at the Second Battle of St. Albans. Margaret's forces were triumphant, sending Warwick away from London and rescuing King Henry VI from the Tower of London. Warwick's troops retreated and joined with Edward's own army marching north to Yorkshire.

Edward marched into London after the victory at Mortimer's Cross and proclaimed himself king of England on March 4, 1461. At that point, most Londoners had grown to dislike Margaret of Anjou, an ambitious foreigner whom they had never warmed to. The court did not make it difficult for Edward to seize the empty throne. Queen Margaret was not willing to let go of power so easily, however, so she rallied and sent her troops to chase down Edward's when they went to reclaim York in mid-March. The two sides clashed many times before meeting a final time just north of Towton, Yorkshire.

Both armies camped nearby the town of Towton on March 28, preparing for battle in the morning. It was unusual for a battle to take place on a religious holiday, but that particular Palm Sunday, the Duke of Somerset and Edward of York lined up a combined 50,000 to 200,000 soldiers. Various contemporary sources and historians do not agree on the number of troops; however, they do agree that this was by far the largest battle of the Wars of the Roses.

The morning of March 29 was cold and snowy, but the battle was not to be avoided. The Lancaster army had significantly more support from the English nobility, as well as a larger number of individual horsemen, spear-throwers, archers, and swordsmen. The Lancaster side was led by a cousin of King Henry's, Henry Beaufort.

The king himself, with Queen Margaret and Prince Edward, was safely settled at York. The York army was led by teenaged Edward of York himself.

The armies met between Towton and Saxton, with the Lancasters given an early advantage in placement. They were protected on two sides by marshlands and a steep riverbank. Safe, the king's men waited for Edward to make the first charge. York's archers let loose in the direction of the wind, but they were eventually beaten back by an immense force of Lancastrians pushing south.

The Plantagenet king's army kept its overall advantage for several hours in the snow, but mid-way through the fight, York's troops were joined by their final contingent, led by the Duke of Norfolk. Positioned such as they were, the king's men could not see the incoming ranks of fresh soldiers until they were nearly upon them. Strong-armed from the rear, the Lancastrian troops lost their grip on the battle.

After up to ten hours of fighting, small contingents of the king's army began to flee, tossing their heavy helmets, shields, and armor aside to escape more quickly. Seeing they'd won, the Yorkists had no mercy for the Lancaster troops. Runaways, surrendered nobles, and captives were slaughtered as they saw the cause was lost and tried to save their own lives. By the thousands they ran across the river, crushing the bridge, with many drowning, and soon afterward, they began climbing over the piling bodies of their own troop. Records from that day reported 28,000 casualties.

Their forces overcome, the deposed King Henry VI and Queen Margaret of Anjou, with their son Edward, ran for shelter in Scotland. Edward had won the throne and was crowned Edward IV, King of England on June 28 that same year.

In the following letter from royal supporters to Queen Margaret following the Towton clash, the queen was advised not to attempt to leave her safe place in Scotland before they arrived. The letter's authors did not deign to address Edward IV as "King:"

To the Queen of England, in Scotland.

Madam, please it your good God, we have since our coming hither written to your highness thrice; the first we sent by Bruges, to be sent to you by the first vessel that went into Scotland; the other two letters were sent from Dieppe, the one, by the carvel in the which we came; and the other, in another vessel; but, madam, all was one thing in substance, of putting you in knowledge of the kings your uncle's death, whom God assoyl, and how we stood arrested, and do yet. But on Tuesdey next we trust and understand we shall up to the king your cousin germain. His commissaries, at the first of our tarrying, took all our letters and writings, and bear them up to the king; leaving my Lord of Somerset in keeping at the castle of Arques; and my fellow Whityngham and me (for we had safe conduct) in the town of Dieppe, where we are yet. But on Tuesday next we understand that it pleaseth the said king's highness that we shall come to his presence: and are charged to bring us up Monsieur de Cressell, now bailiff of Canse and Monsieur de la Mot.

Madam, ferth [fear] you not, but be of good comfort, and beware that ye adventure not your person, nor my lord the Prince, by the sea, till ye have other word from us; in less than your person cannot be sure there as ye are, and that extreme necessity drive you thence. And for God's sake the king's highness be advised the same; for as we be informed the Earl of March is into Wales by land, and hath sent his navy thither by sea. And madam, think verily, we shall not sooner be delivered but that we will come straight to you, without death take us by the way; the which we trust he will not, till we see the king and you peaceable again in your realm; the which we beseech God soon to see, and to send you that your highness desireth.

Written at Dieppe, the 30th day of August [1461]

Some of the casualties of that long-ago battle were discovered in a mass grave in Towton in 1996. After careful archeological excavation and record-keeping, the Towton Skeletal Collection of 43 almost-complete bodies was taken to the University of Bradford for preservation. The bodies show tell-tale signs of extreme violence indicative of the use of war hammers, polearms, knives and swords. Further archeological exploration in the area revealed multiple mass graves as well as the single grave of a presumed noble knight. Further scientific studies are ongoing.

The emotion, drama, fear, violence, and death that marked the decades of war in 16th-century England has left an unforgettable archeological and political legacy. It is even said that the spiritual world bears permanent scars from the terror of those gruesome battles. Many visitors to Towton, for example, have reported sightings that mirror those of the long-ago fight between Edward of York, Richard Neville, and the royalist House of Lancaster. At least one visitor to the historical battlefield has captured paranormal images on film.

The decisive battle in which Edward of York took the crown from Henry VI has provided physical researchers with a treasure-trove of knights, soldiers, buckles, and arrowheads – but its supposed metaphysical properties are more difficult to study. The battle took place in a blizzard at the end of March in 1461, 14 years before Henry Tudor took the throne of England, and believers in the paranormal claim that every year, a similar snowfall hits Towton. They say that if visitors peer far into the snow, they see a massive army fighting the same battle in the name of England's long-dead king. The battle lasts several hours as knights on horseback and foot soldiers meet their deaths again and again.

A pub near the ancient battlegrounds of the Yorks and Lancasters claims to be the regular haunt of a poltergeist. The spirit moves heavy objects, throws kitchen pots and tools on the floor, and pushes over large pots of vegetables that have been left safely level on the stove. Pub owners say the ghost is not malevolent, but very active and generally troublesome. Unable to communicate with the spirit, they simply call it "Nancy."

Nancy isn't the only supernatural being reputedly left behind by the Wars of the Roses. The Cock Beck – the stream in which thousands of soldiers drowned, froze, and were crushed to death under the feet and corpses of their own comrades-at-arms – has its own stories to tell. The innocent-looking stream of water was a major feature of the Battle of Towton, cutting huge lines of men off from freedom in the last hours of the siege. It ran red with blood and was dammed with bodies by the time Edward had won his victory.

People who live near the Cock Beck say some days they can hear the moaning and screaming of dying and injured soldiers who passed away centuries ago. Such tales may be difficult to prove, but they hold great significance for those who believe in them and want to honor the memory of the tens of thousands that died fighting for both sides during the Wars of the Roses. All the ghosts of the battlefield, in their own way, contribute to an ongoing memorial and respect for that bloody and dangerous era in English history.

Chapter 8 – York Takes the Throne

The country's first York king was crowned on June 28, 1461, at Westminster Abbey. It was two days after Edward's triumphant return to London. Immediately upon entering the capital city, King Edward IV called together Parliament and knighted 32 of his most loyal supporters.

While Henry and Margaret remained in Scotland along with some of their exiled English allies, the king had all slain Lancastrian nobility posthumously stripped of their rank and holdings. This act thereby took all privilege, property and income from the families of York's murdered enemies. The Lancastrians and allied families who remained alive were given the chance to change sides or face the same fate. In this way, Edward removed his remaining opposition at court, bullied his cousins into showing respect, and elevated the Yorks and his greatest non-familial supporters to positions of high rank.

There were still hold-out factions of Lancasters in the north, but this was expected and the rebellions were kept relatively under control by the new king. With peace in place throughout the bulk of the kingdom, Edward IV chose to focus on the consolidation of his fractured land. It meant a great deal to the nobility and the commoners alike that Edward had been officially crowned and the bloodiest part of the war was at an end. By the time the Lancaster king was deposed, the country had suffered for six years to provide constant arms, food, supplies, and soldiers to both the Yorks and the Lancasters. Great cities like York and London had come under fire so often that their gatekeepers were loath to open up for anyone, no matter their rank. Finally, most of the country could focus on healing, settling down, and prospering. Moreover, Edward was a young, strong, tall and seemingly intelligent man whose figure commanded a room. He was well-liked.

While Edward IV and Richard Neville, Earl of Warwick, effectively ruled England, the exiled monarchs in Scotland coordinated with northern allies in England and Wales. Margaret never rested, causing clash after clash in the northern region that sapped much of Edward's resources. He and Warwick discussed entering Scotland and facing their enemy once more, as proven by this letter from Warwick to the king in October of 1463. The letter, written by Warwick to the king, expresses the former's satisfaction at the monarch's decision to invade Scotland, and promises to do whatever is necessary to make that campaign successful:

> *My most dread soveraigne lord, aftre humble recommendacion to your good grace. Please it the same to wite yesterday I received your most noble lettres delivered me by your humble subgiet maister .N. whereby I understande to the greate and special comfort and reioysing of me and all your trewe subjiettes in thise parties that your highnesse is purposed towardes this contrie with your mighti powair tothentent tentre into Skotland for the subduyng of your adversaries there. Whiche purpose I beseche our lord ye may bring tagood and aworshipful coclusion aftre thentent of youre most noble acourage and so I doubte nat with Goddis mersy ye shal to the grettest comforte and wele of alle your trew subgiettes of this your roialme and perfite tranquilite of*

the same and utter confusion and distruccion of your said adversaries. So that your said highnesse be purveyde of suche thinges as is necessarily required for the sure and siker perfourmyng of your saide noble purpose, that is to saye of sufficiant victaile by the see to serve your people during the tyme of your abode in the said Scotlande, and to be sure that the said victaill be before you. Also that your said highnesse have with you sufficient stuff of all maner artillerie, that is to saye grete gunnes for beting of places and other gunes for the felde, suffycient powdre, stones and all othre stuffe for the same, grete quantitie of bowes, arows, stringes, speres and all othre habiliments of werre, sufficient nombre of men for ordinaunce as gonners and othre. Without the whiche provision afore your coming, it is thought, undre your most noble correccion, to the lords and men of reputacion in thise parties that inno wise ye shulde come but rathre differre your most noble purpose to such tyme as ye may be sure of the said provision, and yif your said highnesse be purveide as is abovesaid that it may like the same thenne to come, and I trust in our lord ye shal have as worshippful a journay as ever had enyt of your most noble progenitours. Beseching humbly your good grace to geve credence to the berer of this, and to certifie me your most noble pleasire in the premisses to thentent that yif your hignesse come over, I may make me redie tawaite upon the same and warne all your subgiettes in thise parties to do the same, wherto I dar say they wilbe as wel willed to their powair as eny subgiettes that ye have lyving. God knowith, whom I beseche ever to preserve you in joieux prosperite and victorieux felicite.

Writen with my simple hand at your town of Newcastell, your trewe and humble subgiett and liegeman Richard Warrewic

Indeed, after three years being safely hidden by allies in Scotland, Henry VI was removed to northern England because of fears that Edward's negotiations with the Scots would go badly for him.

Several small battles ensued between the diplomatic party and the Lancaster king's protectors. In 1464, Henry VI was captured by Edward and brought back to London. He was locked in the tower once again, with Margaret and his son back in Scotland. He stayed there for five years while the deposed queen continued to rally small groups of armed Lancaster allies at every opportunity.

Chapter 9 – The King in the Tower

Henry Lancaster languished in his luxurious prison. Like his imprisonment under Richard of York, the true king of England seemed pleased enough to do the bidding of Edward IV and did indeed consider the usurper a close friend. Whether this was only his attitude during moments of dementia and delusion, or whether Henry truly felt comradery with his kidnappers, neither history nor contemporary sources can say. It does seem telling that Henry VI made no large effort to free himself or to negotiate with his jailor. It was his meek and mild manner that had cost him many loyal supporters throughout the years of the war, but without Queen Margaret to rally him, Henry was unwilling or unable to change his temperament.

Called the "Mad King" due to his random bouts of dementia, the deposed king would have been considered unsuited for his royal position even if he'd enjoyed constant sanity. Extremely devoted to Catholicism, Henry disliked blood and violence, had no desire to torture or kill enemies, and considered nudity in men or women lewd. His empathy made him quick to forgive debts to the crown. He also used much of his treasury's money to help alleviate the poverty of his people, a fact that would be remembered by them much later.

During his time as king, unfortunately, Henry's methods for ruling the realm were overwhelmingly unappreciated.

Said his 15th-century biographer:

He was a man of pure simplicity of mind, truthful almost to a fault. He never made a promise he did not keep, never knowingly did an injury to anyone. Rectitude and justice ruled his conduct in all public affairs. Devout himself, he sought to cherish a love for religion in others. He would exhort his visitors, particularly the young, to pursue virtue and eschew evil. He considered sports and the pleasures of the world as frivolous, and devoted his leisure to reading the scriptures and the old chronicles. Most decorous himself when attending public worship, he obliged his courtiers to enter the sacred edifice without swords or spears, and to refrain from interrupting the devotion of others by conversing within its precincts.

He delighted in female society, and blamed that immodest dress, which left exposed the maternal parts of the neck. "Fie, fie, for shame!" he exclaimed "forsooth ye be to blame." Fond of encouraging youth in the paths of virtue he would frequently converse familiarly with the scholars from his college of Eton, when they visited his servants at Windsor Castle. He generally concluded with this address, adding a present of money: "Be good lads, meek and docile, and attend to your religion."

He was liberal to the poor, and lived among his dependents as a father among his children. He readily forgave those who had offended him. When one of his servants had been robbed, he sent him a present of twenty nobles [a type of coin], desiring him to be more careful of his property in the future, and requesting him to forgive the thief. Passing one day from St. Albans to Cripplegate, he saw a quarter of a man impaled there for treason. Greatly shocked he exclaimed "Take it away, take it away, I will have no man so cruelly treated for my account."

Henry VI had been extremely popular due to his name and the legacy of his family, but on a personal level he was not well-liked. Henry was awkward, soft-spoken and many found him quite feminine. He did not conform to the men's fashions of the times, notably dressing in plain clothes and avoiding the upturned shoes preferred by other gentlemen of the court. The boastful and self-aggrandized behavior of most European monarchs was polar opposite to Henry's kind and unimposing manner. Essentially having been a political prisoner from his first year of life, it is possible that Henry VI was predisposed to following the orders of stronger, more authoritative members of the royal house.

King Edward provided his docile rival with food, clothing, and a personal chaplain with whom to say the Catholic Mass. He could receive some visitors, but many of those only wanted to spy on the Mad King for their own curiosity.

While locked away, the gentle king wrote poetry. His words expressed his belief that the hunger for riches and power was a dead end in life. After being little but a political pawn his whole life, it is not particularly surprising that Henry VI merely sat back in his comfortable prison and allowed those around him to make decisions. It was the same power dynamic he'd learned in childhood and continued to accept in his marriage.

The following is a poem written by the imprisoned, philosophical king:

> *Kingdoms are but cares*
>
> *State is devoid of stay,*
>
> *Riches are ready snares,*
>
> *And hasten to decay*
>
> *Pleasure is a privy prick*

Which vice doth still provoke;

Pomps, imprompt; and fame, a flame;

Power, a smoldering smoke.

Who meanth to remove the rock

Owst of the slimy mud

Shall mire himself, and hardly scape

The swelling of the flood.

To his credit, King Edward IV could easily have chosen to kill Henry, but was satisfied at having him locked away. His decision to keep the deposed king in the Tower seems to solidify his father's statement that he was never an enemy of King Henry VI, but an enemy of those who advised him. Edward may have kept Henry alive for the simple fact that Richard of York had no intentions of killing him, or he may have worried that Henry's death would reflect badly on him personally. It may have been as simple as that Edward didn't truly see Henry as a threat—after all, the man was content to read and write and keep to himself.

Few records exist from Henry's time in the Tower of London, but it seems he caused little trouble and did as he was told. Five years after he was taken hostage, his people came for him.

Chapter 10 – The Kingmaker Repents

Richard Neville had been dubbed "The Kingmaker" after the series of battles that led Edward IV to the English throne; unfortunately, Neville did not enjoy the same close relationship with the young Duke of York as he had with Richard Plantagenet. Though they were great allies in the early years of Edward's reign, the friendship turned sour after 1464.

With Henry Lancaster safely within his reach, Edward IV looked to other issues facing the kingdom. Continued war with France was something the new king wanted to put his military might into, but Warwick preferred to call a truce and perhaps arrange a marriage between the nations. Warwick visited France and made an effort to cultivate friendships there, but when he accompanied King Louis XI's ambassadors back to Edward's court, the English king was blatantly disrespectful. This sticking point was the beginning of a rift between King Edward IV and the man who had been his father's staunchest ally.

The Earl of Warwick held out some hope that his king would concede to marry a French noble and cement peace between the two nations. Though Edward showed no inclination to do so, it was still a shock when the king married Elizabeth Woodville, a widowed English aristocrat with two sons. Not only was the marriage unadvisable in Warwick's view, but Edward had married in secret without even consulting him. It was the ultimate insult and signified a final break between the two who had fought the Lancasters side-by-side for so long. Neville realized his great influence over the king was all but gone, and he did not take the news with grace. Instead, he accused the new queen of witchcraft.

Edward never forced Warwick out of court, but the latter spent less and less time there. In 1467, Warwick left court long-term and returned to his lands in the north of the country; he was considerably disappointed in how things were going under the York monarch. King Edward, for his part, focused on forging a powerful relationship with the leader of Burgundy as well as his wife's family. To that end, he arranged a marriage between his own sister Margaret and the new Duke of Burgundy, with plans to invade France with his new allies. When English troops entered France the next year, they captured Jersey for the king, but overall, the campaign was considered an incredible waste of money.

In London and beyond, the Earl of Warwick was becoming more popular than the man he'd placed on the throne. He knew it, too. In 1469, Neville decided he had enough and officially switched sides. Warwick betrayed King Edward IV in favor of the deposed royals he had been fighting for 15 years. He started by orchestrating a royalist rebellion in the north of England, where Henry Lancaster's supporters had yet to be suppressed successfully. It wasn't just another fight because this time Neville had made it personal against King Edward. He'd started negotiating with the king's younger brother, George, and convinced the royal sibling to marry Isabel Neville, Warwick's own daughter.

The rebellions culminated in the battle of Edgecoat Moor on July 26, 1469, and it forced Edward to flee when many of his top supporters were killed. Seizing the moment, the Earl of Warwick offered refuge to Edward that equated to imprisonment. Mere months later, Edward was released and returned to London due to intense pressure from York's supporters. The infighting was still not finished, however. At the Battle of Losecoat Field on March 12 of the next year, Warwick's side lost, and he was forced to retreat to France.

Warwick's presence in France marked an important moment in the history of the wars, since at this point the Earl met with King Louis XI and negotiated a formal alliance with Margaret of Anjou. He returned to England to head the Lancaster army with the help of Jasper Tudor in October 1470. They successfully ousted Edward from the seat of power and forced his retreat from England. Edward fled to Burgundy, while Warwick took Henry from the Tower and placed him back on the throne. Henry VI was crowned again and paraded through London for everyone to see.

To further entrench himself into the royal family, Neville arranged the marriage of his daughter Anne to Edward Lancaster, Henry and Margaret's son. By that time, the heir to King Henry was 16 years old. Anne was thirteen.

The reversion to Lancaster rule was incredibly short-lived, as was Warwick's regained power.

Edward had gone to Burgundy, where he enlisted the support of Charles, heir to King Louis XI of France. With French investments on his side this time, Edward returned to England via the north. When he was recognized, he pleaded that he'd only come back to take back his York estate. The Percy family, greatly influential in that part of the country, owed much of their land to the Yorks and let Edward pass.

Reestablished in his estate, King Edward set out to find his old friend Warwick. Edward convened with his brother George, who had changed sides again once it became obvious his father-in-law never intended to put him on the throne. It was George who attempted to speak with Warwick when the two parties met near Coventry.

George Plantagenet couldn't convince his one-time ally to concede defeat and accept Edward as his king. Diplomacy having failed, the York brothers turned around and raced towards London. Upon their departure, Warwick summoned his own allies and set off in the same direction.

The gates of the capital city swung easily open for their returning king since residents of the city much preferred Edward to the feeble Lancastrian. Henry VI, so briefly removed from his cushioned prison, was promptly returned to the Tower of London. There was no struggle, not even an argument. Henry VI, apparently pleased to see his cousin Edward, offered himself to the usurper and stated pleasantly how he trusted himself to York's custody completely. Having dealt with the old king, Edward set back out to end further rebellion from Warwick.

Chapter 11 – The Battles of Barnet and Tewkesbury

Both sides prepared for an important clash, but they avoided attack until they had been joined by their full forces from all parts of the country. It took several weeks of pacing the countryside before the armies were sufficiently populated.

The battle commenced on April 14, 1471, when over 20,000 soldiers gathered, ready to fight. King Edward IV met the Earl of Warwick near Barnet, Hertfordshire, about twelve miles north of London. The Yorkists, dressed in blue and red livery, were outnumbered two to one. Warwick's forces, which included the king's own brother George, wore red.

The battlefield was covered in thick fog when the front lines woke before sunrise and prepared to fight. Royal and rebel forces were spread across multiple fields separated by hedgerows, so movement was somewhat restricted. Edward attacked first, firing arrows despite the fog that clouded the archers' view. Attacking with archers first was a classic military strategy designed to take out as many members of the opposing side as possible before engaging in hand-to-hand combat. The Yorkists loosened thousands of arrows upon the Lancastrians, reaching over 350 yards per shot.

On Warwick's side, troops were confused by the fog. The lack of visibility was bad enough, but there was a ripple of paranoia through the ranks that crippled the morale of Warwick's army. Many of his soldiers and battalion leaders were worried about further side-changing on the part of their allies-at-arms. It was a poor start for the Lancastrian force, which at one point began to mistakenly attack itself due to the similar banners under which each army marched. Observers of the friendly-fire attack called "Treason!" believing that the Earl of Warwick had crossed over to the York side on which he used to fight.

In the confusion, the Lancastrian army backed away from the clash in search of visual perspective and a chance to communicate with its own factions. Seeing his enemy's forces slow, Edward sent in the reserve soldiers for a fresh wave of slaughter that ultimately caused overwhelming backpedaling from Warwick's army. After fighting for six hours, Richard Neville himself, the Kingmaker and traitor to Edward IV, was caught and killed by the opposing army. Though artwork celebrating the battle showed King Edward murdering his traitorous friend, that is unlikely how it happened.

At the death of their leader, the Lancastrian army broke up and went into full retreat. Both sides lost about 1,500 people, but when the battle was over, the Lancasters still hadn't given up the cause. Queen Margaret of Anjou, her son Edward, and Edward's wife Anne Neville arrived in England the same day the battle took place. Though their defeat had been brutal, the queen's presence rallied the remaining Lancaster army. Those who hadn't deserted marched through the west country and into Wales to recruit once more. When they entered England again, they were met by King Edward and his army for the last time at Tewkesbury, Gloucestershire.

Margaret had done a fine job of recruiting throughout the southwest, but it was to her advantage that Jasper Tudor still had a strong army of Welsh soldiers at her disposal. The loss of Richard Neville had been a crushing blow to the Lancastrians, but they would not give up the fight so long as there was an available Lancastrian heir to the throne. As far as they were concerned, Henry VI and his son Edward were meant to rule England: it mattered not how many battles were fought, or if there were others who might try to claim the throne. The Lancastrian case had become considerably more compelling now that Prince Edward had reached the age of majority.

Now 17 years of age, the son of Margaret of Anjou and Henry VI had a personal vendetta against the Yorks for dethroning his father and taken away his own birthright. He fought with the Lancastrian forces under the leadership of the Duke of Somerset.

Margaret intended for her army to storm the city of Gloucester before facing Edward of York's forces, but the latter sent a message to the city's governor ordering him to keep the gates shut. Denied entry to the city, Margaret decided it would be a waste of resources to fight her way in so the deposed queen rerouted her troops to nearby Tewkesbury. The unplanned extra ten-mile hike exhausted the soldiers, but Edward's troops were also overworked by their rapid chase. On the night of May 3, the Lancastrians camped outside Tewkesbury, and the Yorkists just three miles away.

The River Avon and the Severn were to the Lancastrian's rear; an ancient earthwork fort encompassed Margaret's camp, though the queen herself retreated to a distant church for safety before the battle began the morning of May 4. In front of the Lancastrian army lay a jumble of hedgerows and difficult terrain that the enemy would have to cross.

As was his habit, Edward of York advanced first. He had placed spearmen in the adjacent woods, and these surprised Somerset's section as they tried to surround the Yorkist's left flank. The Lancastrians lost ground and attempted a retreat that proved difficult across the Severn River. Somerset, furious at one of his colleagues, Wenlock, for failing to come to the rescue, killed the man in question before escaping.

Again, Margaret's forces were in full retreat, with many drowning as they tried to reach nearby churches and hide inside. York's men pursued viciously, rounding up the men in churches and killing each one. They saved some of the Lancastrian lords for public execution days later, placing their heads on pikes.

The Prince of Wales, Edward Plantagenet-Lancaster, had been killed during the battle. His mother hid for several days in mourning before sending a message to King Edward that she was at his mercy. She had no hope of restoring her fragile and disinterested husband, Henry VI, onto the throne of England, and without her son and heir, she felt the Lancastrian cause was lost. King Edward took the fallen queen into London and kept her as a prisoner and war trophy.

Chapter 12 – The Death of a King

Edward of York had won an important victory and it seemed there was no one left with the adequate authority to challenge him. Both Henry VI and Queen Margaret were in his custody, the rival Prince of Wales was dead and the traitorous Earl of Warwick was dead. It was a glorious part of the new king's saga and one that was touted fiercely by his family and supporters.

There were still Lancastrians in Wales under Jasper Tudor and rebellions in the north, though without Queen Margaret or Prince Edward to lead them, their dislike of the York king was of relatively little consequence. Centered in Kent, however, was one more haphazard pro-Lancastrian army posed to strike. It was led by Thomas Neville, illegitimate cousin to the Earl of Warwick.

Neville was in possession of several ships and had been patrolling the English Channel during his cousin's military campaign. After the death of Richard Neville at the Battle of Barnet, the remaining Neville pieced together an army with his soldiers at sea and the unhappy people of Kent. He sailed to London via the Thames with artillery and a massive army of 20,000. Orchestrating two attacks, first at the London Bridge and the second at Kingston upon Thames, Neville put everything he had into wresting control from York. The fighting took place between the 12th and 15th of May, 1471.

King Edward's protectors in London fought Neville off fiercely, firing back across London Bridge with their own artillery and ultimately capturing thirteen of his ships. Thomas' last stand was unsuccessful and he was beheaded on the 22nd of September.

The very same night Edward returned triumphantly to his capital city, King Henry VI died in the Tower of London. An anonymous person, identifying themselves only as "a servant to Edward IV," heralded by the king as a hero and wrote a document celebrating Edward's final victory. It was heavily-laden with York propaganda, touting the worthiness of Edward over his enemies and Henry VI. It referred to Thomas Neville as the "Bastard" and claimed that the old king in the tower died of "melancholy."

Historie of the Arrivall of Edward IV

Here is it to be remembred, that, from the tyme of Tewkesbery fielde, where Edward, called Prince, was slayne, thanne, and sonne aftar wer taken, and slayne at the Kyngs will, all the noblemen that came from beyond the see with the sayde Edward, called Prince, and othar also theyr parte-takers, as many as were eny might or puisaunce. Qwene Margaret, hirselfe, taken, and browght to the Kynge; and, in every party of England, where any commotion was begonne for Kynge Henry's party, anone they were rebuked, so that it appered to every mann at eye the sayde partie was extincte and repressed for evar, without any mannar hope of agayne quikkening; utterly despaired of any maner of hoope or releve. The certaintie of all whiche came to the knowledge of the sayd Henry, late called Kyng, being in the Tower of London; not havynge, afore that, knowledge of the saide matars, he toke it so great dispite, ire, indingnation, that, of pure displeasure, and melencoly, he dyed the xxiij. [23rd] day of the monithe of May. Whom the Kynge dyd to be browght to the friers prechars at London, and there, his funerall service donne, to be caried, by watar, to an Abbey upon Thamys syd, xvj [16] myles from London, called Chartsey, and there honorably enteryd.

The Kynge, incontinent aftar his comynge to London, taried but one daye, and went with his hole army, aftar his sayd traytors into Kent, them to represse, in caas they were in any place assembled, and for to let them to assemble by any comocion to be made amongs them, wher unto they, heretoforne, have often tymes bene accustomyd to doo. But, trwethe it was, that they were disperbled as afore; but the sayd bastard of Faucomberge, with great nombar of mariners, and many othar mischevows men, called his sowldiours, or men of were, went streyght to Sandwyche, and there kept the towne with strengthe, and many great and small shipps, abowt xl and vij, in the haven, all undar his rule. And, as sone as they undarstode the Kynge and his hoste aprochid nere unto them, the sayd bastard sent unto hym suche meanes as best he cowthe, humbly to sew for his grace and pardon, and them of his feloshipe, and, by appoyntement, willed there to be delyveryd to the Kyngs behove all his shipps, and became his trwe liegemen, with as streight promiyse of trew legiaunce as cowthe be devised for them to be made, whiche, aftar delyberation taken in that parte, for certayn great consyderations, was grauntyd. Wherefore the Kynge sent his brothar Richard, Duke of Gloucestar, to receyve them in his name, and all the shipps; as he so dyd the xxvj. [26th] day of the same monithe; the Kynge that tyme beinge at Cantorbery.

And thus, with the helpe of Almighty God, the moaste glorious Virgin Mary his mothar, and of Seint George, and of [all] the Saynts of heven, was begon, finished, and termined, the reentrie and perfecte recover of the iuste title and right of owr sayd soveraygne Lord Kynge Edward the Fowrthe, to his realme and crowne of England, within the space of xj wekes; in the whiche season, moienaunt the helpe and grace of

Allmyghty God, by his wysdome, and polyqwe, he escaped and passyd many great perills, and daungars, and dificulties, wherin he had bene; and, by his full noble and knyghtly cowrage, hathe optayned two right-great, crwell, and mortall batayles; put to flight and discomfeture dyvars great assembles of his rebells, and riotows persons, in many partyes of his land; the whiche, thwoghe all they were also rygorously and maliciously disposed, as they myght be, they were, netheles, so affrayde of the verey asswryd courage and manhod that restethe in the person of our seyd sovereigne lord, that they were, anon, as confused. Whereby it apperithe, and faythfully is belevyd, that with the helpe of Almyghty God, whiche from his begynning hitharto hathe not fayled hym, in short tyme he shall appeas his subgetes thrwghe all his royalme; that peace and tranquilitie shall growe and multiplye in the same, from day to day, to the honour and lovynge of Almyghty God, the encrease of his singuler and famows renoume, and to the great ioye and consolation of his frinds, alies, and well-willers, and to all his people, and to the great confusion of all his enemys, and evyll wyllars.

Here endethe the arryvaile of Kynge Edward the Fowrthe. Out of Mastar Flyghtwods boke, Recordar of London.

Historians generally agree that King Edward sentenced the deposed king to death and had one of his trusted supporters carry out the sentence in secret. It is generally believed that King Henry VI was struck heavily on the head while he kneeled to pray in his chapel. His body was exhumed in 1910, and it revealed blood and hair stuck to the skull.

Chapter 13 – The Final Plantagenet Kings

There is much speculation about why King Edward would kill Henry VI after having happily kept his rival in the Tower of London for so many years before. Perhaps he was simply finished with quashing endless rebellions and believed that by cutting down the final Lancastrian with claim to the throne, his rule would gain balance and peace. It could also be true that Henry had been kept alive so long to negate the potential of his more powerful son, Prince Edward. As long as Henry was alive, Edward may have felt capable of overcoming his enemy; perhaps the younger and more fearsome Prince Edward seemed a challenge that was bigger than necessary. Once the threat of Prince Edward had been eliminated, there would have been no reason to keep his father alive.

King Edward IV enjoyed a relatively normal reign once the Lancasters were finally beaten, and he settled into his role with gusto. There were two military campaigns that occupied the remaining years Edward spent on the throne: the alliance with Alexander Stewart of Scotland, and the invasion of France with the support of the Duke of Burgundy.

Desiring a friendly relationship with Scotland, Edward decided the best means accomplish that goal was an alliance with the brother of King James III. Alexander Stewart wanted to replace his brother James on the throne of Scotland, and if Edward would support him with troops, supplies, and money, the two could become firm allies. Edward went ahead and sent his brother Richard, the Duke of Gloucester, north; the mission was a huge success. Gloucester took the capital city of Edinburgh and captured King James III.

Unfortunately for King Edward and Gloucester, Alexander Stewart lost his nerve and reneged on his deal. James was released and England retreated, but not before the Scottish king was forced to hand over Berwick-upon-Tweed. The city had changed hands before, most recently when Queen Margaret had gifted it to Scotland in exchange for the safety and support of her family in 1461.

As for France, Edward found himself allied with another fickle ruler. The Duke of Burgundy failed to provide military support for England's invasion of France, forcing King Edward to negotiate a treaty with King Louis XI.

In his younger days, King Edward had been a pinnacle of health and strength. He was over six feet in height, taut and lean, and ready for battle at a moment's notice. In the later 1470s, however, he spent less time on the battlefield and more on the throne. He seemed to be making up for the extreme violence and exertion of the early years of his rule by sitting back and delegating. He was much less active, gained quite a bit of weight, and suffered from a succession of illnesses.

Despite his failing health, King Edward made some distinctive changes to the kingdom for which he had fought so hard to rule. He reached out to the disgruntled Welsh and made much of naming his son and heir the new Prince of Wales. He rebuilt St. George's Chapel at Windsor, patronized artist and printer William Caxton, and created an impressive collection of books and illuminated texts.

Centuries later, Edward's library went on display at the British Museum.

Edward never quite recovered from the constant threat of treason by those he trusted, which led him to execute his brother George in 1478 following the latter's involvement in yet another conspiracy. Many others were executed for similar reasons.

King Edward became seriously ill in April of 1483, though the reason is lost to history. Some sources claim typhoid, some pneumonia. Whatever the reason for the illness, Edward worsened as the weeks wore on and realized that he needed to take a final look at his will. His son, Prince Edward, was named successor, but the king's brother Richard was named Lord Protector of the young heir. Edward IV died on April 9, making 12-year-old Edward V the new king.

When the elder Edward died, his heir and brother were away from London. The two convened twenty days later at Stony Stratford, and immediately Richard had his nephew's retinue arrested and sent away to await beheading. Richard Grey, one of Queen Elizabeth Woodville's sons from her first husband, was among those who lost his life on Richard's instructions.

When Richard took young Edward V into his personal possession and instructed the boy to follow his orders, dowager Queen Elizabeth Woodville fled with her remaining children to Westminster Abbey.

Edward V traveled with his uncle to London, at which point the young king was placed in the Tower of London—not only a traditional prison for important prisoners, but the traditional place for kings to lodge before their official coronation. Probably unaware that his servants and friends had been sent to their deaths, Edward V would not have thought twice about following and trusting his father's brother. He stayed in the Tower and awaited his coronation, planned for June 25. Two weeks before the coronation was supposed to take place, Edward's younger brother, Richard, was taken from his mother on the premise that he was needed at the ceremony. Richard was placed with the child king in the Tower.

While the children awaited the coronation, an argument raged between the nobles of London that concerned their legitimacy. The proposed illegitimacy of the boys came from the revelation that King Edward IV had been engaged to a woman called Eleanor Butler before he married Elizabeth Woodville. At the time, engagement to be married was binding and no other marriage could take place afterward without the dispensation of the church. Richard Plantagenet pushed this fact on Parliament, who officially claimed both boys illegitimate on the very day Edward V was meant to have been crowned king of England.

In his nephew's stead, Richard Plantagenet became king of England under the title Richard III. He was crowned on July 3, 1483.

Chapter 14 – Richard III and the Princes in the Tower

Technically, Edward V was the reigning king of England from April until July. His kingship was officially stripped from him after Richard convinced Parliament of the invalidity of his parents' marriage at the end of June. Not allowed to attend their uncle's coronation, Edward and Richard seem to have remained in the Tower of London for the rest of their lives. Once they were deemed unnecessary to Richard's rule, the princes simply stopped being seen. They made no visits, attended no royal events and after several weeks no longer received visitors.

John Argentine, a doctor who served the royal family, called on Edward V and his brother several times during the summer of 1483. Though contemporary accounts claim the boys were seen from time to time that summer, eventually they faded from the public altogether. By the end of the year, they were assumed dead. Historians generally agree that Richard III murdered his nephews Edward V and Richard; however, there is no concrete proof for or against him. Other suspects have been named, including Richard's successor, Henry VII.

Dominic Mancini, an Italian visitor to the English court in the summer of 1483, was captivated by the mysterious events surrounding the princes in the Tower. He wrote about his experiences afterward:

> *But after Hastings was removed, all the attendants who had waited on the king were debarred access to him. He and his brother were withdrawn into the inner apartments of the Tower proper, and day by day began to be seen more rarely behind the bars and windows, til at length they ceased to appear altogether. The Physician John Argentine, the last of his attendants whose services the king enjoyed, reported that the young kin, like a victim prepared for sacrifice, sought remission of his sins by daily confession and penance, because he believed that death was facing him.*
>
> *I have seen many men burst into tears and lamentations when mention was made of him after his removal from men's sight; and already there is a suspicion that he had been done away with. Whether, However, he has been done away with, and by what manner of death, so far I have not yet at all discovered.*

No satisfying explanation concerning the whereabouts of either Edward or Richard was ever given. Richard knew perfectly well that his courtiers and the English commoners believed he'd killed the young boys for the crown – but he neither confirmed nor denied the rumors. It would have been simple just to bring the boys out in public to quell suspicion, but again, nothing of the sort was arranged. There were no declarations of death and no funerals, which allowed several young men in the following years to fake their identities as both Edward and Richard.

Thomas More, a philosopher, clergyman, and lawyer who would become an advisor to King Henry VIII, wrote his own account of the incident, claiming to have witnessed several connected events after the deaths. He reported that the boys' bodies were buried under a pile of stones at the foot of a staircase within the Tower complex. According to More's story, years afterward the bodies were moved by a priest and placed into a grave more fitting to a king and his brother. The location of the grave was forgotten, since the man who commissioned the priest to move the bodies, Sir Robert Brakenbury, died soon afterward.

A century later, two small sets of bones were found during a renovation of the White Tower. These were inspected and found to match the ages of the princes who disappeared. The bones were placed into a large urn and interred at Westminster Abbey where they rest to this day. More sets of similar bones have been uncovered in the years since, but no conclusions have been made concerning the identity of the remains or the manner of death. Queen Elizabeth II has never given her approval for the interred bones at Westminster to undergo DNA and other forensic testing.

Richard III's wife, Anne Neville, died in 1485 before the couple could have any more children to replace their deceased heir, Edward. No one knew better than Richard how important it was to have a son waiting in the wings to take over the throne, and rumors flew around London that he planned to marry his niece, Elizabeth of York. Elizabeth was the daughter of King Edward IV and the sister to the mysteriously lost princes in the tower. Such a marriage would have been a clever political move, since it would connect the deposed Lancaster line with his own York line.

Queen Elizabeth, the younger Elizabeth's mother, had every reason to want to destroy Richard Plantagenet. Not only had Richard III taken the throne from family but he had imprisoned and probably murdered both of her sons. Hearing that Richard III planned to wed her eldest daughter must have been unbearable.

Before any such plans could move ahead, King Richard was forced to defend his crown from the one remaining man who could make the same claim on it: Henry Tudor. Tudor's campaign was heavily influenced by his mother, the dowager Queen Margaret Beaufort. Margaret had always harbored ambitious plans for her son, to whom she was very close. Once every opponent to Richard III had been eradicated from the fabric of the kingdom, she saw the chance for her son to make the great leap from hard-working nobleman to king of the realm.

Margaret was not the only dowager queen to believe in her son's potential. Elizabeth Woodville, fearing further tragedy for her family and desiring revenge, wanted Henry Tudor to succeed as well. The two women met and plotted together to challenge Richard. They did not have to wait long for their plans to come to fruition. Only three years into his rule, King Richard III faced Henry Tudor on the battlefield. Tudor was joined by Queen Elizabeth's eldest son, Thomas Grey, half-brother to Edward V. Grey had joined a failed rebellion in October 1483 and was as loyal as his mother to the new hope of the Lancaster line.

Chapter 15 – The Battle of Bosworth

Richard III's son and heir, Prince Edward, had died at the age of ten in 1484. If he died without further issue, the crown must revert to the closest male heir. With no Yorks or Lancasters left of the Plantagenet dynasty to make a claim, the closest remaining heir came from a Welsh nobleman who had married the dowager queen of England, Margaret Beaufort: Henry Tudor.

Henry Tudor was born in 1457, a nephew to the Mad King Henry VI. His father, Edmund Tudor, was half-brother to Henry VI, making Henry Tudor a Lancastrian relation. Jasper, an important figure in the Wars of the Roses, was Henry's uncle; Owen Tudor, a casualty of the Battle of Mortimer's Cross, was his grandfather.

With the support of two dowager queens, France, and much of the nobility, Henry Tudor made his campaign for the throne. His first attempt, in the same year Richard III claimed the throne, was unsuccessful since a strong storm stopped his ships from crossing the English Channel. Based in Brittany and then in France, Tudor waited until everything was ready to strike again. He set out at the beginning of August 1485 and arrived on Welsh soil on the seventh day of the month. Wales being the ancestral home of his father's family, Tudor found himself very welcome. King Richard's own appointees in south Wales gave up their positions to follow Henry eastward. As he and his troops moved towards the English capital, Henry gathered more support and soldiers along the way.

King Richard was alerted to the impending army and so gathered his own forces promptly. The royal army marched north and met Henry Tudor's troops near Bosworth Market, Leicestershire. They were midpoint between the eastern and western shores of England. The Lancaster side had 5,000 to 8,000 soldiers—half of which were likely French—and the Yorks slightly outnumbered them. Thomas and William Stanley, the latter of whom had married Henry Tudor's mother Margaret Beaufort, gathered thousands of their own loyal troops but refused to declare a side before the battle began. Such moves were customary of the Stanleys who preferred to join the winning side just in time to claim victory and save themselves great sacrifice. They had, however, met secretly with Henry Tudor twice as he swept the countryside looking for more men.

The two armies finally met on August 21. King Richard's troops were positioned to the northeast upon Ambion Hill, while Henry Tudor's were spread along the plains to the southwest. The two sections of the Stanley's army were positioned some distance southeast of Henry's; Richard could see them from his hilltop camp. The problem for the Stanleys, who did seem to hope for a Tudor victory, was that Richard had kidnapped Thomas' son prior to the battle for leverage. In preparation for the battle, King Richard sent a message to the Stanleys advising them to join his army or expect Thomas' son to be killed. Another message came from Henry, asking his mother's husband to formally declare a side.

In answer to Richard, Thomas replied simply that he had more sons. To Henry, he said he would join once the battle plan had been laid out and the fighting started. Both sides had to begin without any certainty where the extra 2,000 to 4,000 soldiers would end up. With no other choice, Henry's side advanced under the leadership of the Earl of Oxford, a man with much more battlefield experience than Henry.

The fight started with cannon fire and arrows loosed by the Yorkists on the hill. They had the immediate advantage given their position, but Oxford was experienced and clever about the art of warfare. The Lancastrians huddled together instead of breaking apart into the traditional three-piece battalion and marched steadily towards higher ground, sending their own deluge of arrows into the opposing side. Once the lines met in hand-to-hand combat, Oxford gained the advantage.

To the northeast of the central battle lay Richard's flank, led by the Earl of Northumberland. Perched on a nearby hill, Northumberland's men were not in a good position to reinforce the king's soldiers; however, Richard signaled to them to do just that. The flank remained where it was, leaving the king to find a different solution. Seeing Henry Tudor within reach, Richard rushed towards him. He knew that if he struck down the leader of the rebellion, the Lancastrians would retreat.

On horseback, Richard charged with a retinue of mounted knights towards his foe, killing Tudor's standard bearer. Henry jumped off his horse and retreated to the relative safety of his bodyguards on the ground, making himself a less conspicuous figure. With Richard separated from his main army and grappling with Henry's bodyguards, the Stanleys decided it was time to show themselves. Their troops raced in and joined the Lancastrians, pressing Richard back until he was unhorsed and thrown into a marsh.

Richard III refused to surrender although he was pressed on all sides by enemy forces. Rhys ap Thomas, one of the Welsh noblemen who defected from his position to join Henry Tudor, is reported to have killed the king while he struggled to find footing in the slippery marsh. At his death, the York army slowly abandoned the battle as they learned their king was gone. Richard's crown was retrieved from the marsh.

In the instant that King Richard III was slain, the kingdom was left without a ruler; Henry Tudor knew it was essential to make his claim immediately or others may deign to take the throne before he returned to London. To cement his triumph and the beginning of his rule, Henry arranged a humble coronation as soon as the king was killed.

When the fighting was finished and the vanquished army had flown, Henry rode into the nearby town of Stoke Golden, surrounded by his commanders and closest supporters. There, they mounted a hill and stopped beneath an oak tree, where Henry kneeled and was crowned with the battered golden circlet taken from Richard III's helmet. He stood, proclaimed King of England by Lord Stanley, and all around him cheered loud and long enough to be heard by the men who remained on the battlefield. That hill was named Crown Hill thereafter, and still exists today – though it has been developed into a residential area.

Henry had the bodies of all those slain during the battle brought to nearby St. James Church to be buried. Richard III's body was not treated so kindly. Tudor did not allow his enemy a Catholic burial, but instead had Richard's body stripped and put on a horse so he could take it to the city of Leicester as proof of his victory. After two days, the body was unceremoniously buried at the church of the Greyfriars, without so much as a marker.

The following is King Henry VII's public proclamation after the Battle of Bosworth:

Proclamation of Henry Tudor:

And moreover, the king ascertaineth you that Richard duke of Gloucester, late called King Richard, was slain at a place called Sandeford, within the shire of Leicester, and brought dead off the field unto the town of Leicester, and there was laid openly, that every man might see and look upon him. And also there was slain upon the same field, John late duke of Norfolk, John late earl of Lincoln, Thomas, late earl of Surrey, Francis Viscount Lovell, Sir Walter Devereux, Lord Ferrers, Richard Radcliffe, knight, Robert Brackenbury, knight, with many other knights, squires and gentlemen, of whose souls God have mercy.

Upon his return to London, Henry Tudor was publicly proclaimed king of England under the title Henry VII. He organized a formal coronation on October 30, 1485 and was hailed as the first non-Plantagenet ruler in three hundred years.

Chapter 16 – The Foundation of the Tudor Dynasty

In claiming the throne of England, Henry Tudor knew that he needed to be different than his predecessors. He wanted all the people of England to accept his rule, including both parts of the Plantagenet line. His first order of business, following the coronation, was to marry Elizabeth of York, daughter of King Edward IV and Queen Elizabeth Woodville. Since Henry's claim to the crown was through his mother, great-great-granddaughter of King Edward III of House Lancaster, he wanted to cement his position by joining the York part of the family with his own. Elizabeth and Henry were married on January 18, 1486, at Westminster Abbey.

Elizabeth and Henry's children would be equally Lancaster and York, the ideal solution to the Plantagenet feud that began over three decades of civil war in England. To celebrate the bringing together of the split family, King Henry VII designed the Tudor Rose: a simple floral emblem whose inner petals were white and whose outer petals were red. It was a symbolic end to the war of the York white rose against the Lancastrian red rose.

Henry's rise to the throne was not without its detractors, though his victory on the battlefield in 1485 is marked by most as the end to the Wars of the Roses which had impoverished the realm and turned cousin against cousin for 30 years. The Tudor king met a few more armies in battle before his reign was through. Each rebellion centered around a supposed Plantagenet claimant to the throne, including a man who said he was the younger of the lost princes in the tower. King Henry's forces squashed the rebellion, and Henry had the boy installed in the palace kitchens. Another potential claimant, the son of George Plantagenet, was lodged permanently in the Tower of London.

With the diminishing rebellions under control, Henry VII focused on peace treaties with his neighboring nations, as well as bringing sorely-needed funds into the royal treasury. The king created a very effective taxation system and raised a great deal of money for infrastructure projects such as Europe's first dry-dock at Portsmouth. He invested in the creation of an English navy and sent ships to the Ottoman Empire to purchase alum—a mineral important to the wool and dyeing industries—and resell it throughout Europe and England.

King Henry VII was very intent on keeping his family safe, healthy, and happy. He remained very close to his mother, who had borne him at the age of 13 and helped him earn his place on the throne. Henry's letters to Margaret were doting and indicative of the love the king had for his wife and children as well.

Madam, my most enterely wilbeloved Lady and Moder, I recommende me unto you in the most humble and lauly wise that I can, beseeching you of your dayly and continuall blessings. By your Confessour the berrer I have reseived your good and most loving wryting, and by the same have herde at good leisure such credense as he would shewe unto me on your behalf, and thereupon have spedde him in every behalve withowte delai according to yowr noble petition and desire, which restith in two principall poynts: the one for a generall pardon for all manner causes: the other is for to altre and chaunge part of a Lycense which I had gyven unto you before for to be put into mortmain at Westmynster; and now to be converted into the University of Cambridge for your Soule helthe, &c. All which thyngs according to your desire and plesure I have with all my herte and goode wille giffen and graunted unto you. And my Dame, not onely in this but in all other thyngs that I may knowe should be to youre honour and plesure and weale of youre salle. I shall be as glad to plese you as youre herte can desire hit, and I knowe welle that I am as much bounden so to doe as any creture lyvyng, for the grete and singular moderly love and affection that hit hath plesed you at all tymes to ber towards me. Wherfore myne owen most lovyng moder, in my most herty manner I thank you, beseeching you of your goode contynuance in the same. And Madame, your said Confessour hath more over shewne unto me on youre behalve that ye of your goodnesse and kynde disposition have gyven and graunted unto me such title and intereste as ye have or ought to have in such debts and duties which is oweing and dew unto you in Fraunce by ye Frenche Kynge and others, wherfore Madame in my most herty and humble wise I thanke You. Howbeit I verrayly hit will be ryght harde to recover hit without hit be dryven by compulsion and force, rather than by any true justice which is not yet al we thynke any convenyant tyme to be put in execution. Nevertheless it hath plesed you to gyve us a good interest & meane if they woull not conforme thayme to rayson and good justice to diffende or offende at a convenyant tyme when the caas shall so require herafter. For such a chaunce may fall that thys your graunte might stande in grete stead for a recovery of our Right, and to make us free, wheras we be now bounde &c. And verrayly Madame, and I myht recover hit at this tyme or any other, Ye be sure ye shulde have your plesure therin, as I and all that God has given me is and shall ever at youre will and commaundment, as I have instructed Master Fisher more largely herin, as I doubte not but he

71

wolle declare unto you. And I beseeche you to sende me youre mynde and plesure in the same, which I shall be full glad to followe with Goddis grace, which sende and gyve unto you the full accomplyshment of all youre noble and vertuous desyrs. Written at Grenewiche the 17 day of July, with the hande of youre most humble and lovynge sonne.

H. R.

King Henry VII remained on the throne until his death from tuberculosis on April 21, 1509, 6 years after the death of his beloved wife Elizabeth. His mother died two short months later. The Tudor king's son succeeded him without incident at the age of 18 as King Henry VIII. The first Henry Tudor ruled England for 26 years, giving his kingdom the peace, stability, and time it needed to prosper.

Chapter 17 – Attempts on the Tudor Throne

King Henry managed to stabilize the kingdom, but his rule was not without its own challenges. His detractors claimed he was an illegitimate son of Margaret Beaufort and therefore unqualified to claim the crown. Still others claimed they were Plantagenet survivors whose ties to the kingdom preceded the Tudor kings. The most notorious attempts to gain power while Henry VII wore the crown were made by two young men called Perkin Warbeck and Lambert Simnel. Each claimed to be one of the multiple lost Plantagenet heirs who had vanished after imprisonment in the Tower of London.

Lambert Simnel was the first to make his claim as Edward Plantagenet, though the idea really came from his tutor. The early details of Simnel's life are largely unknown, though he is believed to have come from an average middle-class family who might have been bakers or tradespeople. Born around the same time as Edward Plantagenet, son of George Plantagenet, brother to King Edward IV, Simnel was ten years old in 1487 when he came under the tutelage of a priest called Richard Simon.

Upon becoming acquainted with his young pupil, Simon decided to forego priestly training and instead get Lambert ready to make a noble appearance at court. The priest taught Lambert how to act, think and speak like a member of the royal family, an idea born of the teacher's assertion that his pupil greatly resembled the lost sons of King Edward IV. His initial plan was to have Lambert imitate the younger of those princes, Richard, but by that time it was commonly rumored that both princes had died in their luxurious prison. So, Simon had to make a contingency plan that focused instead on the son of George Plantagenet.

Edward, son of Richard III's brother, had been imprisoned immediately after Henry VII killed the old king at the Battle of Bosworth. The boy was denied the title of Earl of Warwick, which had been promised him by Richard III, and simply kept in the Tower for the same reason as Richard had imprisoned the sons of his elder brother. Henry VII probably hesitated to kill the young Plantagenet outright. Therefore the king decided to keep him within arm's length.

Under Simon's tutelage, Lambert learned his lessons well and went along with the charade. Most of the kingdom knew well enough that the boy was in the Tower, so the priest told everyone around him that Edward had escaped his prison. When the rumor caught on, Simon took his student to Ireland and produced him for the appraisal of the large York contingent there. Lambert Simnel was immediately embraced by the Plantagenet supporters there, including the powerful Earl of Kildare, leader of the Irish government.

Once Simon had cultivated the support of the Irish, his plan to usurp the English crown via Lambert moved swiftly. Kildare vowed to send an army to defeat Henry VII and put Edward in his place. In celebration, the imposter was hoisted on someone's shoulders and paraded through the streets. On the 24th of May, 1487, the false Edward Plantagenet was crowned Edward VI, King of England and Ireland, at the Christchurch Cathedral in Dublin. While the Irish army was gathered, Margaret of York (daughter of Edward IV), and

York relative John de la Pole gathered supporters in England and Germany. De la Pole went so far as to say he'd assisted the imprisoned Plantagenet in his escape.

Only two years into his hard-earned reign, Henry Tudor knew first-hand how simple it was for one faction to overthrow another. Forewarned about the upcoming challenge, he quickly gathered his own army and prepared to meet his foe in battle. It was the beginning of summer when John de la Pole returned to England with his gathered troops. The two armies met on the 16th of June near Newark, Henry at the head of 12,000 soldiers and de la Pole at the head of 8,000. The battle lasted about three hours, after which de la Pole and about half of his troops were dead.

It was the first time Henry was forced to defend his throne with military might, and he could not afford to lose. Though the king realized it was hardly the fault of Lambert Simnel, he punished the peers who had risen against him by stripping them of their lands and titles and removing their heirs from the peerage succession. The ambitious priest, Richard Simon, was sent to a bishop's prison for life. As for Lambert Simnel himself, after a brief turn in prison he was put to work in the castle kitchens. The real Edward Plantagenet was briefly removed from the Tower and shown to the public to prove he was still very much alive. Afterward, he was quickly returned to the Tower of London and remained there until 1499, where he met the next major challenger to King Henry VII: Perkin Warbeck.

It is impossible to accurately depict the early life of Perkin Warbeck, since there are two conflicting tales that he told about himself. The first and most controversial identity Warbeck gave himself was that of Richard of Shrewsbury, the youngest of King Edward IV's sons. It seems most likely that Warbeck was born in a continental European country, then brought by his family to Ireland as a child. English may not even have been his first language.

In 1490, Perkin made his first official claim to the English throne while in Burgundy, a region of France ruled by the York family. He claimed that he had been in hiding since his brother, Edward V, was killed in the Tower of London, and that he had been spared from death because of his very young age. After making his royal claim, Warbeck traveled to Ireland to garner support for his cause. As with Lambert Simnel, the Irish were captivated by the teenager who claimed to be a Plantagenet heir to the English throne. In fact, Warbeck once claimed that it was the Irish who convinced him to act the part of Edward IV's lost son – though such a statement clashed with the boy's own timeline.

Though the Mayor of Cork was happy to lend support to Warbeck as Richard of Shrewsbury, Perkin's case didn't find the traction he was hoping for. The young man returned to Burgundy where the real Richard's aunt, Margaret of York, took him in and taught him the ways and manners of the English court. She unofficially gave him the title of Duke of York, a name by which he was known throughout Europe. Perkin met a great many nobles and members of royal houses while under the care of Margaret, some of whom went as far as to call him King Richard IV.

While the supposed Duke of York sheltered in Burgundy, King Henry VII kept tabs on his whereabouts and activities. Henry complained to the Duke of Burgundy, but his request to have the man extradited was ignored. In retribution, Henry imposed a trade embargo on the duchy and prohibited commerce between the two nations. Burgundian support of the supposed Duke continued.

Thanks to European support, by 1495 Perkin Warbeck had earned himself the attention of several English peers. These peers personally visited the Duke of York in Burgundy, then colluded to develop a plan of attack against Henry VII. The Tudor king was well forewarned, however, and as many as a dozen English Lords were found and arrested on his behalf. They were tried, found guilty of treason and ultimately sentenced to execution – however many had their sentence changed to imprisonment and fines afterward.

Warbeck and Margaret of York were still hopeful even after losing their English contingent. That same summer, the pretender to the throne sailed to Kent at his aunt's expense, in search of more support. Instead, the troops he brought with him were attacked by royalists upon landing. Before Warbeck even disembarked, he was forced to retreat to Ireland, where this time he was more popular than he had been upon his first visit. He used the momentum to invade Waterford, but failure there led him to quickly flee to Scotland.

King James IV of Scotland was just as welcoming to the alleged Duke of York as the nobility and rulers of France and the Holy Roman Empire had been. With Henry VII arranging a marriage between his son Arthur and the daughter of Spain's most powerful monarchs, James IV was eager for a friendlier English connection, especially one who was on good terms with France. Warbeck even married a member of the Scottish aristocracy, Catherine Gordon, before conspiring with the Scottish king to invade England.

Warbeck was clearly grateful for all the favors granted him by the Scottish king and his lords, as indicated by his overwhelming statements of gratitude. In a letter to his bride-to-be, he gushed about her beauty and charm:

> MOST NOBLE LADY, IT IS NOT WITHOUT REASON THAT ALL TURN THEIR EYES TO YOU; THAT ALL ADMIRE, LOVE, AND OBEY YOU. FOR THEY SEE YOUR TWO-FOLD VIRTUES BY WHICH YOU ARE SO MUCH DISTINGUISHED ABOVE ALL OTHER MORTALS. WHILST, ON THE ONE HAND, THEY ADMIRE YOUR RICHES AND IMMUTABLE PROSPERITY, WHICH SECURE TO YOU THE NOBILITY OF YOUR LINEAGE AND THE LOFTINESS OF YOUR RANK, THEY ARE, ON THE OTHER HAND, STRUCK BY YOUR RATHER DIVINE THAN HUMAN BEAUTY, AND BELIEVE THAT YOU ARE NOT BORN IN OUR DAYS, BUT DESCENDED FROM HEAVEN.

ALL LOOK AT YOUR FACE, SO BRIGHT AND SERENE THAT IT GIVES SPLENDOUR TO THE CLOUDY SKY; ALL LOOK AT YOUR EYES AS BRILLIANT AS STARS, WHICH MAKE ALL PAIN TO BE FORGOTTEN, AND TURN DESPAIR INTO DELIGHT; ALL LOOK AT YOUR NECK, WHICH OUTSHINES PEARLS ; ALL LOOK AT YOUR FINE FOREHEAD, YOUR PURPLE LIGHT OF YOUTH, YOUR FAIR HAIR; IN ONE WORD, AT THE SPLENDID PERFECTION OF YOUR PERSON ;—AND LOOKING AT, THEY CANNOT CHOOSE BUT ADMIRE YOU; ADMIRING, THEY CANNOT CHOOSE BUT LOVE YOU; LOVING, THEY CANNOT CHOOSE BUT OBEY YOU.

I SHALL, PERHAPS, BE THE HAPPIEST OF ALL YOUR ADMIRERS, AND THE HAPPIEST MAN ON EARTH, SINCE I HAVE REASON TO HOPE YOU WILL THINK ME WORTHY OF YOUR LOVE. IF I REPRESENT TO MY MIND ALL YOUR PERFECTIONS, I AM NOT ONLY COMPELLED TO LOVE, TO ADORE, AND TO WORSHIP YOU, BUT LOVE MAKES ME YOUR SLAVE. WHETHER WAKING OR SLEEPING, I CANNOT FIND REST OR HAPPINESS EXCEPT IN YOUR AFFECTION. ALL MY HOPES REST IN YOU, AND IN YOU ALONE.

MOST NOBLE LADY, MY SOUL, LOOK MERCIFULLY DOWN UPON ME YOUR SLAVE, WHO HAS EVER BEEN DEVOTED TO YOU FROM THE FIRST HOUR HE SAW YOU. LOVE IS NOT AN EARTHLY THING, IT IS HEAVEN BORN. DO NOT THINK IT BELOW YOURSELF TO OBEY LOVE'S DICTATES. NOT ONLY KINGS, BUT ALSO GODS AND GODDESSES HAVE BENT THEIR NECKS BENEATH ITS YOKE.

I BESEECH YOU, MOST NOBLE LADY, TO ACCEPT FOR EVER ONE WHO IN ALL THINGS WILL CHEERFULLY DO YOUR WILL AS LONG AS HIS

DAYS SHALL LAST. FAREWELL, MY SOUL AND MY
CONSOLATION. YOU, THE BRIGHTEST ORNAMENT
OF SCOTLAND, FAREWELL, FAREWELL.

After the marriage, the mutual invasion went forward. The Scottish troops attempt to enter England commenced in September of 1496, hinging on the assumption that the old Yorkist faction in northern England would rally behind Perkin Warbeck. Only a few days into the campaign, it became clear that no Warbeck troops would materialize. Lord Neville approached with a royal army from the south, and James was pushed back into his own territory. Finished with Perkin Warbeck, the Scottish king sent him back to Ireland. The so-called Duke of York fled back to mainland Europe after bungling another attempt at taking Waterford.

One year later, Warbeck returned to England, this time via the south at Cornwall. He tried to capitalize on their recent revolt against Henry VII's taxes, which were being raised to pay for a war with Scotland. Again employing the guise of Duke of York, Warbeck told the Cornish people that he had an excellent relationship with Scotland and that not only would he avoid war with James IV but he would remove the war tax. He had very good timing, since this was exactly what the Cornish wanted to hear. They hailed Warbeck as King Richard IV and sent him northward with 6000 troops.

At Taunton, Warbeck surrendered to the king's army and was arrested. King Henry put the pretender in the Tower of London until he confessed to being an imposter, at which point the king allowed him the luxury of attending court – still under domestic arrest in Henry's palace. Warbeck was separated from his wife, who was under the guardianship of Queen Elizabeth. After a year and a half under close watch, Warbeck escaped and was quickly recaptured. He went directly to the Tower, where he met a very interesting inmate: Edward Plantagenet, the true Earl of Warwick and false identity of Lambeth Simnel.

By this point, Edward had been living in the Tower of London for 14 years. Aged 24 when he met the false Richard Plantagenet, it is believed that Edward was suffering from a mental illness.

Both men knew they had little chance of gaining the king's favor at that point, so they conspired to make a getaway. They made their attempt in 1499, but failed, after which they were sentenced to be executed. Warbeck was hanged on November 23; Plantagenet was beheaded for treason on November 28.

The final Yorkist heir was born just five years before King Henry VII died: Richard de la Pole. Richard was brother to John de la Pole, named heir to Richard III who swore an oath of allegiance to Henry Tudor. Richard had some degree of respect in France and Scotland, with whom he planned to invade England in order to put himself on the throne in 1523. Though he gathered as many as 12,000 troops to fight against Henry VIII, the war never took place. Before he could organize ships and take advantage of good weather, Richard de la Pole was killed at the Battle of Pavia where he fought on behalf of Francis I of France.

The death of Richard de la Pole in 1525 ended the York hereditary line, since he had no sons and only one illegitimate daughter. It could be said that with his death, the Wars of the Roses were truly ended. Having fought off multiple challengers, both the first and second Henry Tudor ensured the succession of their own line.

Chapter 18 – The Sainthood and Cult of King Henry VI

The gentle goodness of King Henry VI was not forgotten after his death, even though he spent only 15 of his 49 years truly ruling the kingdom. After the Earl of Warwick, Prince Edward, and finally Henry VI were killed in the Wars of the Roses, people unwilling to support a York monarchy spoke often of the goodness of the old king.

Sympathy for Henry VI intensified following his funeral since attendees claimed the old king's body bled during the service. According to medieval superstition, this was a sign that Henry had been a victim of foul play, for it was believed that a murdered body would bleed anew to betray the violence it had endured. The people of England lamented the loss and apparent brutal end to the Plantagenet line of kings, and in King Henry VI found the ideal subject for their own religious obsession. Almost immediately, a niche portion of English society chose Henry as their lost savior and saint.

When Henry Tudor took the throne of England, he realized that people would love and accept him more readily if he showed his own heavy lament at the loss of Henry VI. The dead king had been, after all, Henry's own half-uncle, and both Henry and his mother knew how important it was to show respect and reverence for rulers of the past. Henry Tudor showed his respect for Henry VI by building a chapel at Windsor Abbey to hold the remains of the king who, by that time, people overwhelmingly believed to have been murdered. With both Edward IV and Richard III dead, however, there was no one to question on the subject: the true cause of Henry's demise remains unknown.

Henry VII capitalized on the growing cult of Henry VI by allowing the publication of a book of miracles attributed to the dead king, which included more than 300 miracles supposedly performed by the last Lancastrian on the throne. Such miracles began to be reported as soon as the old king was interred in his tomb.

The English public knew very well that their lost king had been incredibly devout, reportedly spending up to an hour in silent prayer whenever he entered a chapel. He had been generous, passive, humble—all the things a devout Catholic was supposed to be. When the idea started to circulate that Henry VI had been murdered and did not simply pass away from depression, his mourners began to believe he was a martyr. They pursued the creation of Henry VI as a saint by the Pope, a goal for which the book of miracles would be evidence.

The miracles of King Henry VI include his supposed curing of a young girl with badly infected lymph nodes. Another person claimed that the king's spirit had raised a girl from the dead after she'd been killed by the plague. Still another report claimed that a man was revived following a public hanging for a crime he did not commit: While his dead body was being carted away, he started to breathe again and escaped. The man said King Henry had protected his windpipe. The bulk of the miracles compiled for the book occurred posthumously.

For the manuscript commissioned by Henry VII, many wonderful stories were collected. One told the story of a boy who fell into the trough beneath a water wheel and became stuck under the water. Nobody present could reach him, nor could any adult fit safely under the wheel. At that point, the old king entered the tale:

Then on a sudden someone chanced to mention the glorious King Henry, and soon they were all invoking his memory with one voice. And so they made a common effort and got the wheel to turn; thinking that perhaps if they did this at least the stoppage of the water would be removed and the dead body might pass out under the wheel in the rush of the stream. To their astonishment the turning of the wheel, with all the violent impulse of the stream, accustomed as it was to move a huge stone with all ease, could not now shift the body of one little child. So at last one of the onlookers, bolder than the rest, jumped into the pool, and by standing there breast-deep managed to catch the boy by the shoulder with an iron hook, and so drew him to land by a providence rather than by skill. He was laid, then, on the dry bank, and all that saw it, finding that the body was cold already, bewailed him with woebegone faces, all hope lost that his breath would come again to him, and the life that had been his...They began to invoke God and his glorious Virgin Mother Mary, sheltering themselves beneath the renowned merits of his champion, King Henry...the breath of life thus suddenly restored to him, he returned not only to life but to perfect health, and grew to full age.

The dead king's hat was placed in his chapel at Windsor Abbey so that Catholic pilgrims might touch it and put it on. The hat became a popular cure for people suffering from migraine headaches. It stayed at the chapel for nearly fifty years, until England's church was reformed by King Henry VIII.

Due to Henry Plantagenet's cult following, the chapel built by Henry Tudor received masses of visitors every year. King Henry VII sent multiple petitions to the Pope in Rome asking for his predecessor to be officially canonized and made a Catholic saint. The paperwork and research were undertaken, but so slowly that by the time a decision might have been reached, Henry VIII had broken with the Catholic Church altogether. Multiple attempts have been undertaken to promote the would-be saint's cause, but as yet none of these has achieved its goal.

In the 16th century, famous playwright William Shakespeare immortalized the events and characters of the three-decade struggle between the Lancasters and Yorks in eight plays that cover the early history of the Plantagenets: "Richard II," "Henry IV Part One," "Henry IV Part Two, "Henry VI Part One," "Henry VI Part Two," "Henry VI Part Three," "Edward V," and "Richard III."

Shakespeare wrote multiple plays about Henry VI that speculated a great deal about his role in the Wars of the Roses, and his ultimate fate. Shakespeare portrayed Richard Plantagenet, still Duke of Gloucester under the rule of his brother Edward IV, as the murderer of King Henry VI. This is what Shakespeare's version of Richard says during the scene where Henry lay dying after being stabbed by his cousin:

I, that have neither pity, love, nor fear.

Indeed, 'tis true that Henry told me of;

For I have often heard my mother say

I came into the world with my legs forward:

Had I not reason, think ye, to make haste,

And seek their ruin that usurp'd our right?

The midwife wonder'd and the women cried

'O, Jesus bless us, he is born with teeth!'

And so I was; which plainly signified

That I should snarl and bite and play the dog.

Then, since the heavens have shaped my body so,

Let hell make crook'd my mind to answer it.

I have no brother, I am like no brother;

And this word 'love,' which graybeards call divine,

Be resident in men like one another

And not in me: I am myself alone...

Triumph, Henry, in thy day of doom.

Chapter 19 – The Legacy of the Wars of the Roses

After being at war with itself for 30 years, England was full of scars, many of which remain to this day. The kingdom's noble houses had been dragged through battle after battle, forced to question their traditional loyalties and watch – often up close – as their family members died violently. Members of the feudal poor suffered in the same way, being constantly forced to fight in support of those who owned the land on which they toiled. The population of the country was negatively affected, as were its basic industries. With able-bodied men away fighting, gardens and crops suffered, harvests were small, and the economy was crippled.

The fact that so many different claims could be made on the crown – successful ones – revealed a fundamental flaw in the monarchical English system. Because the lords of the land had so many people available to fight for them, it was possible for a member of the nobility to raise an army that was larger than the king's. It was a strange reality that meant land workers owed their primary loyalty to the lord of the land, not the monarch. That was exactly why the York family, extensive landowners, could persevere for so long and eventually triumph over Henry VI. Once Henry Tudor took the crown, he actively lowered the number of peerages (lordships, earldoms, etc.) by appointing very few new people to the nobility. As the possessors of such titles grew old and passed away, Henry oversaw a decline in the power of the aristocracy.

The Tudor era represented a much more stable kingdom in which people were able to work their land, ply their trades, and grow the national economy. Increasing population and industry in England following the Wars of the Roses led to an eventual blossoming of art, early sciences, architectural design, and leisure, particularly during the reign of Queen Elizabeth I. Playwrights like William Shakespeare found almost endless inspiration from the wars of the Lancasters and Yorks, while tapestry weavers and painters attempted to depict the moments they considered most significant to history.

Apart from Shakespeare, there are countless writers, spanning centuries, who have brought the history of 15th century England to fascinated audiences in the form of books, historical research, movies, and television series. Characters from the Plantagenet and Tudor dynasties continue to fascinate audiences of Showtime's "The Tudors," BBC's "The White Queen," and readers of multiple novels by writers of historical fiction like Philippa Gregory. Historians, archaeologists, genealogists, and royalists continue to this day to debate the validity of that infamous flurry of claims to the throne, as well as to search for further evidence of what happened to the lost princes Edward and Richard York in the Tower of London.

The physical legacy of the wars persists to this day. In 2012, an archeological excavation of the area that was once the church of Greyfriars in Leicester began. Remarkably, a human body was recovered in exactly the area that had been believed to hold Richard III's remains, under the parking lot of Leicester City Council. The body was a man in his thirties with the same deformed spine that characterized England's last Plantagenet king. Just as telling were the severe head injuries shown on the skull. The team ran multiple tests and concluded that the body they'd discovered was indeed that of King Richard III. Intense debate followed regarding what to do with the king's remains, with a group of apparent Plantagenet descendants desiring to make the decision on behalf of their ancestor. Ultimately, a court made the ruling to keep the old king's body in Leicester.

In March 2015, the king was ceremoniously interred at Leicester Cathedral after being led via funeral procession through the site of the Battle of Bosworth. He reentered the city in a wooden coffin, draped in black velvet and pulled by four horses. Though Queen Elizabeth II did not attend the ceremony, she personally wrote a eulogy for her 14th great-grand uncle Richard and was represented at the funeral by her daughter-in-law Sophie, Countess of Wessex. Several other members of royalty were present, as well as descendants of the Plantagenets, who placed white roses on the coffin. The original site of Richard's burial has been converted into a memorial center in which visitors can view the empty grave through a specially-designed glass floor.

Queen Elizabeth II wrote:

> *The reinterment of King Richard III is an event of great national and international significance. Today we recognize a King who lived through turbulent times and whose Christian faith sustained him in life and death.*

> *The discovery of his remains in Leicester has been described as one of the most significant archaeological finds in this country's history.*

> *King Richard III, who died aged 32 during the Battle of Bosworth, will now lie in peace in the City of Leicester in the heart of England.*

> *I have fond memories of my visit to Leicester Cathedral in 2012 and I am delighted to learn that its re-ordering has been completed in time for the reinterment Service.*

I send my sincere thanks to the University of Leicester, members of the Church and other authorities in Leicester who have made this important occasion possible.

The discovery of Richard's body has opened up the possibility of a large genetics project focusing on the timeline of the many royal handovers during the 15th century. The research conducted so far relies on the collected DNA samples from descendants the House of Plantagenet, who were selected following very precise genealogical studies. Historian John Ashdown-Hill pinpointed one idea candidate: Joy Ibsen, a female descendent of Anne of York, Richard III's sister, living in Canada.

The importance of Joy's connection to the late king's sister was maternal since DNA scientists needed to trace the familial connection through a purely female line. Such a precise relationship to the ancient royal family would preserve the mitochondrial DNA in each successive generation until Joy was born. Though Joy died before the research could be carried out, her son Michael was happy to participate in the research performed by Leicester University. In this case, Joy would have passed her mitochondrial DNA to all children, so the fact that Michael is a male will not pose any problems.

The University sought out a second DNA match through an all-female line, a search that produced Wendy Duldig. Duldig's and Ibsen's genetic samples do indeed show a matching female ancestor. The search for an all-male succession line was more difficult, since Richard III himself left no living heirs. Starting with Richard and Edward's great-great-grandfather Edward III, researchers traced the male lineage up to Henry Somerset, the 5th Duke of Beaufort. Five heirs to the bloodline were located for testing which came up with some surprising results.

Four of the male-line descendants showed Y-chromosomes that matched Somerset, but one had a different type. This means that at some point between Edward III and the Duke of Beaufort, at least one male listed in the family tree was not the father of the children listed as his. Another break was found when comparing the Y-chromosome from a French heir to Edward III.

All this means that at some point in history, the Plantagenet line was falsely recorded at least once – a fact that could impact the accepted royal line of succession today. There is a possibility that the oldest Plantagenet, Geoffrey of Anjou, is in fact not an ancestor of Richard III, the Tudor monarchs or today's Windsors. The royal family's genealogy could be much more muddled than any of us – including the royals themselves – realize.

It's a very ironic ending to a story that began with such strict adherence to genetic lines. And yet, the history of the Plantagenets, the Tudors and their relatives – confirmed by DNA or otherwise – is the collective story of all England, all France and Scotland, all Ireland, and Wales at the end of the Middle Ages. The end of the Wars of the Roses signified the beginning of the Early Modern Age in England, a time when prosperity and civility began to blossom. The 30-year war ultimately strengthened the power of the crown and allowed for much more effective legislation throughout a kingdom that would soon become an unquestioned world power.

That legacy continues today with the House of Windsor.

Here's another book by Captivating History that we think you'd be interested in

Check out this book

And another one…

Check out this book

References

ARMSTRONG, C. A. J. (TRANSLATOR.) THE USURPATION OF RICHARD THE THIRD: DOMINIONS MANCINUS AD ANGELUM CATONEM DE OCCUPATIONE REGNI ANGLIE PER RICCARDUM TER CIUM LIBELLUS. New York: Oxford University Press. 1936.

Bergenroth, G. A. (ed). 'Spain: December 1495', in CALENDAR OF STATE PAPERS, SPAIN, VOLUME 1, 1485-1509, London; 1862.

Blakman, John. Translated by M. R. James. "Henry the Sixth. A Reprint of Blacman's Memoir with Translation and Notes." 1732.

Cheetham, A. The Wars of the Roses. University of California Press. 2000.

CUP Archive, (1923). The Miracles of King Henry VI: Being an account and translation of twenty-three miracles…with introductions by Father Ronald Knox and Shane Leslie.

ELLIS, H. (ED.) ORIGINAL LETTERS ILLUSTRATIVE OF ENGLISH HISTORY, series 1, vol. 1.

Gairdner, James (1880). *Three Fifteen-century Chronicles, with Historical Memoranda by John Stowe,* Camden Society, New Series, Vol. 28.

Hughes, P.L. and J. P. Larkin (eds.) ROYAL PROCLAMATIONS, Vol. I. The Early Tudors (1485-1553.) New Haven, 1964.

Kekewich, Richmond, Sutton, Visser-Fuchs & Watts (eds.) THE POLITICS OF FIFTEENTH-CENTURY ENGLAND: JOHN VALE'S BOOK. Allan Sutton, 1995.

Multiple authors. *Paston letters: original letters written during the reigns of Henry vi., Edward iv., and Richard iii.*

Recorder of London. *Historie of the Arrivall of Edward IV. in England: And the Finall Recouerye of His Kingdomes from Henry VI.* 1471.

Shakespeare, William. *Henry VI Part Three*, Scene 5 Act 6.

Stevenson, Joseph (ed.) *Letters and papers illustrative of the wars of the English in France during the reign of Henry the Sixth, king of England.* Pub. by the authority of the lords commissioners of Her Majesty's treasury, under the direction of the master of the Rolls.

Free Bonus from Captivating History (Available for a Limited time)

Hi History Lovers!

Now you have a chance to join our exclusive history list so you can get your first history ebook for free as well as discounts and a potential to get more history books for free! Simply visit the link below to join.

Captivatinghistory.com/ebook

Also, make sure to follow us on:

Twitter: @Captivhistory

Facebook: Captivating History:@captivatinghistory

Printed in Great Britain
by Amazon

10011655R00061